YOU
ARE
Enough

YOU ARE ENOUGH

An Hachette UK Company
www.hachette.co.uk

Vie Books, an imprint of Summersdale Publishers Ltd
Part of Octopus Publishing Group Limited
Carmelite House
50 Victoria Embankment
LONDON
EC4Y 0DZ
UK

www.summersdale.com

Printed and bound in China

ISBN: 978-1-80007-002-8

Substantial discounts on bulk quantities of Summersdale books are available to corporations, professional associations and other organizations. For details contact general enquiries: telephone: +44 (0) 1243 771107 or email: enquiries@summersdale.com.

YOU ARE
Enough

EMBRACE YOUR FLAWS AND
BE HAPPY BEING YOU

◆

CHERYL RICKMAN

To Brooke,
may you always know
how good enough you are

✦

Contents

INTRODUCTION   8

PREFACE   10

**PART ONE: EXPECTATIONS
                 AND EVALUATIONS   16**

The Pressure of Perfection   18

The Shackles of Should   30

The Comparison Trap   40

The Committee   56

The Inner Critic Challenge   70

PART TWO: GOOD ENOUGH – THE IMPORTANCE OF BALANCE 78

Being Enough   80

Having Enough   90

Doing Enough   100

Looking Enough   106

Feeling Enough   116

PART THREE: SELF   126

Self-Acceptance   128

Self-Belief   134

Self-Compassion   138

CONCLUSION   144

REFERENCES   148

FURTHER READING   150

ACKNOWLEDGEMENTS   151

ABOUT THE AUTHOR   152

INTRODUCTION

The burden of expectation can be relentless. It's this pressure that first sparks our fear of failure, a flame fanned by the expectations of others over time, which can lead us to value ourselves based on our academic achievement or popularity, or both. Increasingly we are all judging our self-worth based on how many "likes" our content gets on social media and fretting about whether we're doing enough, contributing enough and being purposeful enough with our lives, about whether we look good enough or feel happy enough, compared to how everyone else appears to be doing.

The culture of compare and despair has woven its way into the fabric of every level of society – from giant corporations and successful social media influencers to our children and our overwhelmed selves. And it's difficult to put the lid back on the box. Feeling like we don't measure up gets us down. Indeed, not feeling good enough has a lot to answer for. That sense of inadequacy has stolen many a dream, trampled ambitions, sabotaged relationships and is responsible for causing anxious thoughts about where we're headed, judgemental thoughts about what we've done and depressive thoughts about where we are now.

So what can we do about it? After all, we are each so much more than our achievements, our belongings and our looks. The truth, whether you believe it or not, is this: you *are* enough, I am enough, we are enough. So why do we so often feel like we're not, and what practical actions can we take to remind ourselves that we are?

What we need is balance, between appreciation and achievement, between compassion and comparison and between self-improvement and self-acceptance. So this book tackles "the more war" – exploring how modern society has led us to constantly want to do more, have more and be more and how exhausting that is!

It also serves as a reminder that you are not alone in feeling "not enough", in feeling sometimes like an imposter about to get found out. Most people, even those we look up to, have felt this way at some point in their lives. From HRH The Queen and Michelle Obama to the legendary Davids (Attenborough and Beckham).

But there is another way. What if we went about our daily lives knowing we are good enough, accepting our imperfections while using our unique strengths? What if we could find a better balance between appreciating what we have and striving for what we want, and between who we are already and who we wish to become? And what if, rather than comparing ourselves to unattainable and unnatural standards and to strangers on social media, and consequently feeling terrible, we started to look inward, to what we have to be proud about, to our own strengths of character, so we can feel good?

You Are Enough is a book about freeing ourselves from the "shackles of should" which come from multiple sources in society. It's a guide to cultivating an attitude of "enoughness", providing practical ways to turn down the volume on comparison, criticism and expectation and turn up the volume on acceptance, balance and compassion.

Preface

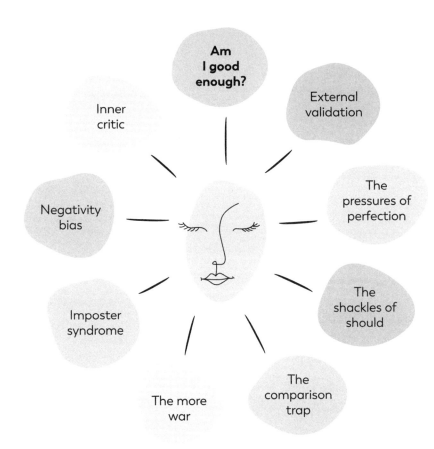

THERE'S SOMETHING YOU SHOULD KNOW

Before we go any further in considering our enoughness, there's something important you should know. I want you to know that the way you see yourself is often distorted. Your own perception of your worth and how others see you is skewed as a result of ancient survival responses. These ancient responses are negatively affecting our modern-day self-worth. Because, when it comes to self-evaluation, our brains are stuck in the Stone Age. The truth is, we are wired to care what other people think of us.

I'm here to tell you that this feeling and belief about not being sufficient as you are – whether occasional or constant – has arisen as a result of some outdated inner wiring that all humans have, wiring that is thousands of years old, which has good intentions and used to protect us, but now leads us to believe inaccuracies, assume the worst and fall into thinking traps which no longer serve us.

Thankfully, it's possible to rewire this ineffective and potentially damaging mental circuitry and recharge negative energy into positive. This book aims to show you exactly how. It's time for an upgrade.

Out with the old

In our cave-dwelling days, when we needed to be part of a tribe to survive, social acceptance and belonging were critical to survival. Back when food was scarce and danger lurked round every corner, we needed to perform well and conform to certain expectations to secure our place, because social disapproval would mean being rejected from the tribe, which could lead to our untimely death.

Back then social approval was everything! It literally meant the difference between life and death. This is why our fear of rejection is a deeply wired survival instinct, an evolutionary trait to keep us safe. Ever since those tribal days when so much was at stake, we've seen rejection as bad and acceptance as good. This explains our in-built need for approval and belonging. We are literally wired to fear failure and rejection and to seek approval and validation because, historically, we needed to belong to a tribe to avoid rejection and ejection from it.

Protective measures

Based on this inherent human need, we measure and assess ourselves and the situations we find ourselves in to help us avoid rejection (and protect us from danger). We do this through the following means:

✦ External feedback (judgement/validation/approval/disapproval).

✦ Inner self-talk (judgement/criticism/negativity bias).

✦ Social comparison (internal assessment of our value in comparison to others).

✦ Social standards or "shoulds" (external expectations).

The resulting evaluation determines our entire self-worth (i.e., whether we feel like we are enough or not enough, adequate or inadequate). This perception impacts how we show up in the world, how we experience our days and what we do with this one precious life of ours. So it's pretty important. However, here's the thing...

The data is distorted, so our self-assessment is too

The data we are basing our self-evaluation on (from the above four methods) is mostly inaccurate, partial, unreasonable and/or negatively skewed. So we are basing our self-worth on incorrect data and telling ourselves stories based on false narratives. Given how important our self-worth is to how we live our lives, this may be quite astounding news! But how exactly is the data skewed? And why is our self-assessment off?

The answers to these questions are what this book shall reveal in more detail, along with clear instructions and easy-to-implement tips on exactly what you can do about it. So you'll be able to rewire the ancient wiring and redress the balance around answering the question "am I enough?" with a resounding yes!

Cause and effect

First though, it's crucial to understand why else this issue of not feeling "enough" exists and where it is rooted. Only then can we dig up those roots and plant new seeds to cultivate a more healthy and helpful mindset, so we may flourish and see ourselves as worthy and wonderful, flaws and all.

The parts that work together to make us all – to varying degrees – feel like we are not enough in the first place are:

✦ The pressures of perfection (*I need to achieve perfection – or near perfection – in order to be accepted, valued, approved of*).

✦ The shackles of should (*I should look/behave/speak like this in order to be accepted, valued, approved of*).

✦ The comparison trap (*everyone else has it all together and is doing/looking/being/feeling better than me*).

These contributors to "not enoughness" work together to create:

✦ Imposter syndrome and a sense of inadequacy (*I'm not good enough and will soon be found out for being so utterly substandard*).

✦ A strong inner critic (*you are not good enough and here's a list of reasons why*).

✦ A preoccupied focus on the future destination (*I will only feel happy and satisfied once I have achieved x and y*).

The good news is, with this information as a wake-up call, it is possible to combat each of these contributors and tackle what they create in us by regaining control over our thought patterns, uncovering what matters most to us and setting our own more authentic standards. That is what this book will explore – each chapter will define the problem, why it exists, and what we can do about it. Because once we know all of this, the better positioned we are to work on the solution.

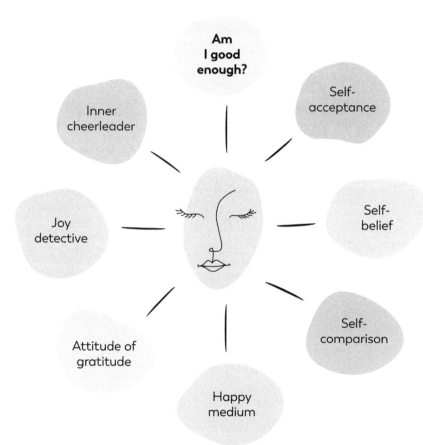

PART ONE

EXPECTATIONS AND EVALUATIONS

Who was I before I became who the world told me to be?

Glennon Doyle

In our modern lives, busy as they are, we tend to accept our beliefs, rather than question them. Yet feeling less than we truly are benefits nobody. Feeling inadequate not only impacts how we live our own lives, it can also influence how those around us show up in their lives too.

We can only tackle this problem through awareness – by recognizing the cause behind the effect, so we may counter those influences which are doing us more harm than good.

We'll start by getting to know the external expectations that impact how we perceive ourselves and the internal (often inaccurate) evaluations that arise as a result.

CHAPTER ONE

The Pressure of Perfection

Perfectionism has seeped deeper into our lives over the past few decades. As the ability to do more, have more and achieve more has escalated, so too have our expectations of ourselves, our children and each other.

Consequently, perfection has been normalized. We're expected to create a life that is super awesome in every way; we're expected to look amazing, have a successful career, a fit body and an exciting social life. We're expected to be constantly blissfully happy, hugely popular and adored by our soul mate. With such great expectations and so much under scrutiny – from our Instagram followers to our romantic status – it's no wonder we may feel overwhelmed. It's exhausting!

As expectations have risen, so too has perfectionism – defined as the refusal to accept any standard short of perfection, striving for flawlessness at all times. A recent study by psychologists Thomas Curran and Andrew Hill,[1] which explored perfectionism across generations between 1989 and 2016, revealed perfectionism has increased by 33 per cent over the last few decades. That's a lot of pressure!

And while not all of us are perfectionists per se, the normalization and pressures of perfection are negatively impacting many of us to varying degrees. Young people in particular have internalized these pressures and experts suggest it's no coincidence that rising expectations coincide with rising mental illness.

Basing self-worth on performing, looking and living faultlessly sets us up for mental turmoil. The expectation of flawlessness can lead to incredibly destructive diseases like anorexia, bulimia and depression, while the expectation of academic brilliance can lead to anxiety and even suicide. Impossibly high expectations are causing considerable harm!

Indeed, anxiety has now overtaken depression as the most prevalent mental health disorder across college campuses in the US, according to a study by the American College Health Association[2] and, in other Western countries, cases of anxiety have been steadily climbing.

Of course, it's in our nature to want to do well and be well, to be our best selves and to achieve our full potential. But diligence, perseverance and conscientiousness are not the problem, because those qualities tend to include a healthy relationship with failure and the knowledge that mistakes and flaws are part of the journey en route to success. There's nothing wrong with wanting to learn and grow and achieve. In fact, achievement is important to our well-being. Self-actualization is a psychological human need. There's no harm in wanting to reach our potential as long as it's *balanced* with appreciation for what we've already achieved and who we already are. Only when striving for success is balanced with acceptance of our natural imperfections (with a decent dose of compassion when things don't go to plan) can we healthily strive for accomplishment.

Sadly, modern life is causing an imbalance. It's not that we're not enough, but that too much is consistently being asked of us and we are internalizing those expectations. As a consequence, not measuring up is bringing us down. Fortunately, it is possible to swing the pendulum back to a more centred and reasonable place. But first, it's helpful to know exactly what we're dealing with.

The pressure of perfection

According to research by Hewitt & Flett,[3] there are three types of perfectionism, each of which can cause high levels of anxiety:

1. Self-oriented perfectionism is when you hold yourself to incredibly strict (often unattainable) standards, avoid failure and are highly critical of yourself.

2. Socially prescribed perfectionism is when you feel under pressure to be perfect based on other people's high expectations and excessive demands of you. It's the belief that you must be perfect in order to avoid rejection and gain approval from your social circle and from those you work for/with. This is the type of perfectionism that is most prevalent in modern-day society.

3. Other-oriented perfectionism is when you expect other people to be perfect, and judge people based on those unrealistically high standards.

We are not all perfectionists, preoccupied with perfection, but we *are* all exposed to the pressure of perfection to varying degrees. This is how the pressure of perfection works:

✦ High expectations: Standards of excellence and perfection are set and imposed on us (by society, parents, peers and the media).

✦ Unattainable: Because actual perfection is impossible to achieve, it's an unrealistic standard and unattainable myth, a great big pretence. We can't *all* be super-awesome at everything. So, in striving to live up to these expectations we set ourselves up to fail.

✦ Derailed by disappointment: This focus on success means we increasingly don't know how to fail well. Our desire to be our absolute best selves has made us hyper-sensitive to criticism, so we have less capacity to learn from our mistakes and grow.

This means we are likely to:

✦ Give up. This fear of messing up can cause us to give up. To reduce the possibility of failure, we stop trying altogether. In doing so we ironically limit our chances of achieving the success we're striving for in the first place because, when we stop trying, we achieve less by default. Giving up stops us from getting to where we perceive perfect to be.

✦ Beat ourselves up for not being good enough and focus primarily on our deficiencies. This fuels our self-doubt, creates low self-worth and makes us less willing to give things another go.

✦ Feel inadequate. We might keep trying but still feel like we're failing because the expectations are so impossibly high and, in relation to others, we feel like we don't measure up.

None of this is good for us! But that's not all. As external approval is so ingrained into us, we have a natural preoccupation with social evaluation. Consequently, we often contribute to this downward spiral ourselves as we perpetuate the perfection myth.

Preserving the illusion of perfection

By posting our own images of lives well lived, we perpetuate the myth that perfection is attainable, that "your life should look as good as mine appears to". Presenting perfection as reality in this way fuels the false narrative of it being attainable.

I hold my hand up to admit I am guilty of this myself. I want to record my best moments so I can reflect back on them and reminisce, so I can retrospectively appreciate them. And while I'm quite open to sharing my own vulnerabilities and flaws, to paint a truer picture, I tend to omit the more challenging stuff because it often involves other people whose permission I do not have to share publicly.

It's in our nature to want to appear successful and happy – to show the world that we are doing well, just as we used to show our parents as kids. "Look at me," we'd say as we tried to leap from a swing. We crave approval. That's one of the reasons we share images of our best selves on social media (rather than share the truth of our difficult journey or the tougher times). In doing so we broadcast to the world we're not just fine, we're doing great! And on goes the brave face.

Yet this facade of fine and illusion of perfection not only perpetuates the perfection myth, it also makes it harder to ask for help and support when we need it. And the more we post images of perfection and perpetuate the perfection myth, the more other people feel they need to raise their game and expectations, and we all become trapped in this never-ending loop of striving for unattainable standards. Crazy, right?

Great expectations: where do they come from?

So why are these external expectations (from parents, peers, society, the media), which pressure us to be impossibly and consistently brilliant, so high nowadays? And why does living up to them matter so much to us, and have such a powerful impact on our sense of self-worth?

Well, when it comes to perfection or simply the notion of being good enough, abiding by these expectations has a lot to do with the meritocratic society we live in. Somewhat annoyingly, we live in a culture that emphasizes excellence and ranks us based on these rather narrow values.

Yet, excellence is just one way to measure worthiness, but so is kindness, contribution and love. Unfortunately, even though we may personally rank people who are exceptionally kind and loving highly in our own minds, society, the media and even schools push perfection and high achievement as the top priority, and it's making amazing, wonderful people feel insufficient.

So much today is measured and given a metric, and whatever is measured can be compared. From the set you're in at school, the grades you achieve in your exams or the number of goals you score in a match, to the number of friends and followers you have on social media and the number of "likes" your posts gain. We are constantly sorted and ranked based on our image, achievements and popularity. This is how the Western world works.

Hierarchies are everywhere too: in the playground based on who can run the fastest or talk the loudest, at the office based on working roles and within the class system based on measures of wealth, such as house size and holiday destinations.

You can rise within these hierarchies. For example, you can be "working class" and gain a good education to propel yourself toward the traditional measures of success such as promotions at work, but all this takes effort.

Of course effort in itself is no bad thing and is worth encouraging in ourselves and our children. Neither is it negative to have a growth mindset, knowing that you *can* improve your skills and strengths with effort. But there is a difference between the healthy pursuit of *achievable* goals and the pursuit of unattainable perfection or unreasonably high expectations. And because we are bombarded with images of seemingly attainable idealism and constantly told we should be doing better than we are, no matter how much effort we put in, we may still feel like it's not quite enough. And that sucks!

The problem with meritocracy is that each of us as individuals is different and meritocracy assumes limited versions of success, which don't account for these differences. To place a higher value on people who look a certain way, have achieved certain goals, or appear to be the happiest – this doesn't stack up, because in placing greater value on those versions of excellence, society is dismissing:

+ the kind carers who contribute so much to society and give so much love on a daily basis.

+ those who struggled in the school system and didn't go to university but have incredible imaginations and work creatively in the arts doing a job they absolutely love.

+ the real human beings who don't feel happy all the time and regularly cry because they are human and because constant happiness is unattainable and unsustainable (i.e., all of us).

Meritocracy dismisses many different versions of what makes a decent human being and what constitutes a good life. When we see perfection for the unattainable standard and myth it is, we can consider whether there might be another way of viewing the world and our own place within it, we can lift the lid on these crazily high expectations and see how our common desire to measure up to them is fraught with contradiction. Here's why: **we can't *all* be above average**!

Being excellent at something is exceptional and yet it has become expected and thus normalized. But wait – if we *all* strive to be above average and achieved that status, above average would become the new "average". But it's not possible for above average to be average. Gah! So we can't *all* be above average. In other words, if perfection was attainable to all, there'd be zero point striving for it because we'd all be perfect and therefore perfection would be... gasp... average! If only we could be happily average, eh? Given this contradiction, it makes far more sense to accept there are lots of things we may be below average at, and that's okay! So what can we do to stop ourselves from buckling under the pressure of perfection?

STEP 1: CHOOSE DIFFERENT METRICS

What if meritocracy's version of what makes us deserving of success and approval is outdated? By defining new measures of what success looks like to us personally (as unique individuals) and setting new standards for ourselves, we can counter society's limited notion of success.

✦ Set your own standards of success. Write a list of your own metrics based on what matters most to you personally. For example, if the love of your family matters most, measure your own success based on whether you made a member of your family smile or feel better today. If contribution and kindness are important values for you, measure your success by how often you've reached out to someone in need. If, in order to care for others, you recognize the importance of taking care of yourself first, measure your success by how much self-care you made time for this week, stick a gold star or smiley face on your calendar every day you show yourself care and reward yourself when you reach a certain number.

✦ What makes you feel alive? Hearing birdsong when you open your windows? Woodland walks? Sofa snuggles? Stunning sunsets and skies? What if we measured our success not by how much we achieve but by how alive we allow ourselves to feel? Try opening your eyes to the smaller moments which give your life joy – for these moments are your life, more than your achievements. Feeling alive is enough.

✦ Use different traits. Replace the ideal of perfection with another trait, such as perseverance, diligence, devotion or flexibility – these are admirable traits and will still help you toward achieving your hopes and dreams in life, but without the pressure. Expectations only do us good when they are motivational rather than stressful.

✦ Set realistic small achievable goals and commit to them. Check in regularly with how you feel in relation to your goals. Do you feel motivated and inspired because they are reasonable and achievable or overwhelmed and unmotivated because they are too challenging? If the latter is true, break goals down into more manageable chunks. It's okay to have ambitious goals but it's good for morale if you break them into smaller achievable mini goals so that you can enjoy the pleasure of ticking them off. Write down smaller action steps you could take – mini wins that take you toward a bigger goal and celebrate each time you achieve those more reasonable outcomes. This way you get to focus on devotion, rather than perfection because you are proving your commitment to regular intentional action. You're equally likely to reach your destination and, if you don't, you'll still have enjoyed the journey. Yay, winning!

STEP 2: LEARN TO FAIL WELL

Fear of failure is so inhibiting; it can stop us in our tracks. But the more you avoid failure, the more you miss out on doing things you might absolutely love. The fear of doing something badly gets in the way of living life, but if you can shift how you view failure and how you respond to it, you can empower yourself to progress, improve and grow.

See failure as feedback

Shift how you view failure and see every mistake you make as a lesson, each failure as a teacher. This will help you shift toward seeing failure as a good thing, as a crucial learning tool to help you do better next time. Ultimately, we're all a work in progress: we try, we fail, we learn, we grow (and repeat). This means the only real failure is to ignore the lessons mistakes offer by repeating them. Failure enhances resilience too. As anyone who has achieved a high level of success (according to the traditional metrics) will tell you: they've learned *more* from their failures than their successes. Take that in for a moment. *We learn more from what we get wrong than from what we get right.* So failures *enable* improvement and growth. What's more, it's better to try and fail than not bother trying at all. Because done is always better than perfect. When you look at it this way and try to do something regardless of the outcome – you have, by default, done enough. Isn't that a relief when you realize it's not the success that matters, it's the trying? Because there is so much gold in that action. In other words, giving something a go means you cannot fail whether you achieve the outcome you'd hoped for or not, because you'll always gain something from trying.

When you fall down, get back up

When you rise again after a fall you show yourself that you can overcome obstacles and deal with difficulties. This is strengthening. You cannot be a failure anyway because, when things don't work out as you'd hoped, there is always tomorrow, there is always hope. Resilience in the face of failure provides strength, hope and motivation. Things get better. Matt Haig is a wonderful example of this. After being on strong anti-depressants and planning his own suicide, Matt Haig is now a global best-selling novelist who gives hope to millions. If you ever feel so down and full of despair that you wonder whether you can get back up, read stories about those who did and get inspired, because you can too.

STEP 3: REVISE YOUR EXPECTATIONS

Expect to be a bit crap when you try new things. Children learning how to walk stumble and fall, over and over again. Not one single kid ever nailed walking first time. They fell and got up again and they looked a bit silly and wobbly, but that didn't matter at all because they were learning. The same is true for every first time we try something new. (You should've seen the first draft of this book! Jeesh!) So give yourself a break and go again.

Level your expectations to expect challenges

The higher the bar is raised the harder it is to reach it and the more scope for disappointment. This doesn't mean we shouldn't ever "reach for the sky" or "aim for the stars" as long as we get used to the idea of failure to avoid getting derailed by disappointment, (see Step 2). Instead, learn to expect the occasional blooper, be prepared for making the wrong decision from time to time and accept that mediocrity and disappointment are a part of life – important parts. Things don't always go to plan. That's life. You already know this. If everything always worked out as we hoped and life was always easy with no disappointments, we wouldn't appreciate it when things did go well. We need bland to appreciate beautiful. We need struggles and adversity to appreciate flashes of joy and wonder. So expecting hiccups and failures, that's all par for the course. Perfection, on the other hand, is not.

STEP 4: EMBRACE IMPERFECTION

Given that popularity and approval are part of the reason we strive to achieve so much, isn't it ironic that we tend to like imperfect people more than seemingly perfect people? Another reason why the pursuit of perfection is rather a waste of time.

Think about it. We tend to adore the flawed hero who is far from perfect, who makes mistakes but learns from them – the most likeable characters in films and books are those who have a lot to learn, who go on a journey and start from a place of imperfection. It's no accident that writers of novels and films give their heroic characters flaws – they do this so that we root for them.

Maaaaan, if only we could root for ourselves in the same way? If only we could be our own flawed hero? Well, perhaps you can.

Remind yourself how endearing imperfections are
Think of all your favourite book and movie characters and think about your favourite friends and family members. What flaws and imperfections do they have? Consider why those flaws are particularly endearing. Perhaps it's because it makes them more relatable, or perhaps it's because you find yourself rooting for them more than you would a super high-achieving and seemingly flawless person?

Accept your own flaws and vulnerabilities

The self-judgement you may feel about your own imperfections doesn't remove your flaws, it just makes you feel bad about them. Your imperfections are what make you human, relatable and likeable. We earn more love and respect from others by being our real, vulnerable and imperfect selves. So what if we stopped trying to be perfect and accepted all our foibles? The reason you love your best friend is because they snort when they laugh and have a habit of forgetting what they're talking about mid-sentence – you love them for those flaws as much as their more charming qualities. You don't love them because of what their face or body looks like, or because they passed their exams, or have a good job. You love them for who they actually are, flaws and all. Isn't it time you extended yourself the same level of love and acceptance?

Start your own perfectionism-backlash movement

Counterbalance the perfection myth by being as true and real as you feel comfortable being. You might even go as far as to share mistakes and epic fails. My friend Marsha Shandur has a Facebook group called I Don't Have My iSht Together Either. Marsha says: "We all walk around thinking everyone else has it together and only we don't." After noticing how social media exacerbates this feeling, she made the group where people can post examples of NOT having it all together to counterbalance this effect. It's incredibly refreshing to share and witness the stressed moments as well as the blessed ones, which promotes a feeling of camaraderie, unity and empathy. Because, at the end of the day, we're all humans navigating the messiness of being human together.

CHAPTER TWO

The Shackles
of Should

High expectations are just some of the things we are told we "should" aspire to. But there are many more shoulds than this. We are told what we should look like, feel like and behave like from an early age in order to fit certain stereotypes and societal expectations. Society sits us down and tells us what we should want, what we should strive for and who we should aspire to be like. We are conditioned into dressing, speaking, looking and striving a certain way.

Some of this behavioural conditioning is necessary to create respectful societies filled with people who are kind, who contribute and who share good values. For example, wearing clothes, being polite to each other and apologizing when we make a mistake. But some of them are old-fashioned, restrictive and unnecessary.

For example, depending on whether we are boys or girls we are told what length our hair *should* be, what toys we *should* prefer to play with and what colours we *should* prefer to wear. Retailers perpetuate these shoulds so much, the choice is literally removed unless parents, teachers and other influencers over young minds give children the choice back, to play with and wear what they wish to, across the whole spectrum of toys and clothes and colours. (I wrote a book about this called *Yes You Can*, inspired by my Spider-Man-loving, soccer-playing, dinosaur-favouring daughter).

As we grow, societal expectations and shoulds are piled on around marriage, parenthood and career success. You *should* get married (ideally to someone of the opposite sex) and *should* have two children. You *should* work hard to achieve your career goals and life dreams. You *should* look like these people that you see in magazines and on TV and have a toned body and eyebrows like this and you *should* strive to look as young and slender as possible. You *should* make sure you have these fashion items and the right thigh gap. These shoulds are constant and unrelenting.

The authenticity assassin

So we tend to become who we think we *should* be instead of who we actually are. Rather than follow our hearts, we follow what others say we *should* do, maybe not always, but often. We either water ourselves down (believing that we're *too* this or that) or we dress ourselves up (believing that we're *not enough* this or that). In doing so, we trade our true selves for the version of ourselves we think we ought to be in order to fit in and be accepted and liked. We become shackled by shoulds, our freedom to be ourselves restricted.

And it happens to us all. In her book, *More Myself*, Alicia Keys talks about the way "fame brought a new form of hiding" and how she found herself dressing and speaking in a way that felt like a "more digestible version" of herself. "Behind the shifting wardrobe, beyond the softening around the edges, there lurked a message: YOU ARE NOT SUFFICIENT AS YOU ARE." This was a message that the record industry reinforced with its "expectation of female flawlessness".

This hiding and masking of our whole selves is something which is going on within workplaces throughout the world as, in order to fit in, people do something which diversity experts call "covering".

According to research by the Centre for Talent Innovation,[4] 37 per cent of African Americans and Hispanics and 45 per cent of Asians say they "need to compromise their authenticity" to conform to their company's standards of demeanour or style. Meanwhile research on women in STEM suggests that acting "like a man" can be advantageous in becoming a leader in these fields. And in our day-to-day lives, we tone down and ham up parts of ourselves to be who we've been told we should be.

This is how societal standards can squish us, how they squeeze the individuality, the beautiful badassery and the self-worth out of us. We start to internalize external "shoulds" and take on these beliefs as our own. Society trains us to essentially be less of who we are so we can become what it expects us to be. Consequently, we end up trading our authenticity for "their" approval.

Ultimately we end up believing things which aren't true. For instance, the person who believes they're not thin or beautiful enough to pursue a career in entertainment, despite being incredibly talented. The person who has been led to believe that being gay is sinful or shameful so keeps their sexuality hidden, despite having so much love to give. The person who believes they are too old to participate in an activity they love despite being at their most joyful when they do.

Well, screw that! I say enough of this perception that we're not enough. Enough not-enoughness! You are enough because you exist; each of us is unique and individual and that makes us wonderful by default.

Unfortunately, what we are *expected* to do and who we are *expected* to become often have very little to do with what *we* actually *want* and who we *truly are*. To quote Jennifer Pastiloff, the remarkable author of *On Being Human*, "Should is an asshole!" Yes, it is! And "should" is also an authenticity assassin. So why on earth do we go along with this? And what can we do to fight back and free ourselves? Well, the first step toward breaking free from the shackles of should and setting our own more reasonable, achievable standards is to understand *why* we care so much about abiding by them. In exposing this truth, we can take action to shift how we respond to the shoulds that restrict us from being ourselves.

The main reason we remain shackled by shoulds has to do with our intrinsic human need to belong. This need can make it difficult to go against all these shoulds and expectations. However, we mistakenly believe that, in order to be approved of, we need to fit in. Whereas true belonging means you are accepted exactly as you are.

You see, fitting in and belonging are not the same. As Brené Brown so wisely suggests, "fitting in gets in the way of belonging". Fitting in is driven by shoulds. It's about being who you think you *should* be in order to fit in. Belonging, on the other hand, isn't about moulding yourself to fit into someone else's standard or ideal. No, belonging is about being who you are, as you are, unapologetically imperfect you, without changing – and being accepted as such.

Being who you think you should be takes away your power. It's exhausting. Being yourself gives you back your power. It's exhilarating. It's time to break free from the shackles of should! Here's how:

STEP 5: SHIFT HOW YOU SEE REJECTION

Not feeling entirely comfortable being 100 per cent ourselves comes from that same wired-in fear of rejection and disapproval, the concern that if we are completely ourselves, people might not like us. And the truth is some won't, some people might find you annoying or too sensitive or too positive or too loud. They might think you're not fashionable enough or witty enough or cool enough, but that's okay, because those people are not *your* people. Those people are not the people who will accept you for who you are.

Just as some people won't like you, some people will, and those who do will like you for all that you are – your qualities and your quirks. So while you'll always be too this or not enough that for some people, you'll be just right for others. Those are your people.

Measuring your self-worth based on other peoples' reactions means that you set yourself up to feel bad about yourself, because you simply cannot please everyone all of the time. That's literally impossible. The truth is, some people will only give you the approval you crave if you fit into *their* box, but that is so limiting and restrictive. Who wants to live life in somebody else's darn box? This is YOUR life, box-free! So be prepared to disappoint and be true to yourself instead, regardless of rejection because, chances are, you may have been looking at rejection all wrong!

What if, rather than seeing rejection and disapproval as something to fear, we saw it as something to celebrate? Because the more people whose cup of tea you are not, the closer you get to finding the people whose cup of tea you *are*. YOUR people, those who see, hear and value you, just the way you are. Hooray!

THE SHACKLES OF SHOULD

Accept rejection as a gift toward choosing belonging over fitting in

Accepting rejection and disapproval as a part of everyday life will help you to pull out the weeds, i.e., those people who don't get you and will therefore not see, hear or value you as you are. So bring on the rejection, baby! Often, rejection says as much about the rejector as the rejected anyway, and with each rejection you get closer to finding the people who understand and appreciate your true self, and surrounding yourself with yaysayers rather than naysayers. That's a gift. So why not see it as one? (Ooh, the amount of angst you'll save.)

Allow rejection to fuel your perseverance

Accepting rejection goes for what you put out into the world as much as how you show up in the world. For example, it's par for the course to have creative projects and ideas rejected. If your work is turned down, it wasn't meant for the place you submitted it to. If your ideas are vetoed by work colleagues, after taking on any useful feedback, rather than giving up on your ideas, either choose to persist or find somewhere your ideas are appreciated. Either way, use rejection as your fuel, remind yourself that J. K. Rowling's pitch for *Harry Potter* was rejected 12 times before someone recognized its brilliance. Imagine if she'd given up after 12 rejections. The much-loved characters would only exist in her imagination and that would be a Hogwarts-sized shame. So keep going and keep being you, because that's how you'll find your true home, both in work and in life.

STEP 6: CHANGE YOUR ENVIRONMENT AND FIND YOUR TRIBE

What if, rather than change yourself, you changed your environment? What if, in shedding the shackles of should, you uncovered who you *truly* are and what you *really* want, and in doing so, found and connected with people like you with whom you feel a sense of kinship? Because being yourself enables you to foster deeper connections with those who "get" you. What if you took some time to find that tribe?

It's far healthier to change who you spend time with (i.e., those who make you feel like you belong) than to change who you are to try and fit in. So, have a little think: who is YOUR cup of tea? Who are you most drawn to and connected with, who makes you feel good and what qualities do they have? For example, some might have a great sense of humour and make you laugh a lot. Others might be warm, kind people who are good listeners and encouragers. Who energizes you and leaves you feeling inspired, motivated and good about yourself? And who drains your energy and leaves you feeling depleted, doubtful and bad about yourself? In which environments do you feel most able to be yourself? Where do you find that you don't need to cover up your quirks? And where can you let your enthusiasm for certain topics really flow without feeling like you have to tone your opinions down? Find or focus on your tribe. Spend more time with those who make you feel most at home and less time with those who don't.

STEP 7: BE FAITHFUL TO YOURSELF

Okay, it's time to stop trading your authenticity for other people's approval and build your own self-fidelity, rather than deserting yourself and surrendering to external shoulds. There is only one should to undertake: Your true self should be based on your own expectations and not external ones. According to palliative care nurse Bronnie Ware in her book, *The Top Five Regrets of the Dying*, the number one regret of the dying is the wish to "have had the courage to live a life true to myself, not the life others expected of me". If this isn't powerful evidence to support releasing the shackles of should, I don't know what is.

It's only by covering up your true self that you do yourself an injustice by not being enough you. When we choose to show up as our whole selves and live in full colour – undiluted, unmasked and real, imperfect but true, we become better able to sense what feels *right* for us, what expectations feel *reasonable* for us and what actions feel *authentic* for us. This makes life so much easier to navigate and so much more enjoyable, because we're using our own compass to navigate.

1. Who are you?

   ✦ What words might others use to describe you and your personality? What characteristics do you have? Feel free to ask people.

   ✦ What skills do you include on your CV?

   ✦ What else are you good at? (Not listed on your CV.) For example, you might be a good listener, or you might be good at noticing how others feel?

2. Who are you not?

   ✦ What do you sometimes feel pressured into doing or being? List any "shoulds" you've experienced over your lifetime.

   ✦ What parts of you do you sometimes exaggerate or cover up to fit in? For example, perhaps you tone down your regional accent depending on who you're with? Or maybe you wear more neutral clothes to play it safe at work despite loving bright and vibrant colours?

   ✦ What things don't you do because you are too bothered about what other people might think/say? Perhaps you often stop yourself from making hilarious observations in case nobody laughs? Or maybe you've decided not to get your Bauer roller skates from 1987 out because you think you're too old and don't want people to stare at you?

3. How do you prefer to spend your time?

   ✦ What lifts you up when you've been feeling down?

   ✦ Which activities spark your interest and engage you so much that you can lose track of time when you're immersed in them?

+ What do you like to do if you have some spare time?

+ What did you used to love doing when you were ten years old?

+ What activities are non-negotiable parts of your day?

+ If you were guaranteed to succeed in any career, what would you try? And, even more importantly, if you were likely to fail, what would you do anyway because you love it so much?

4. What matters most to you?

+ If you only had one week left to live, what would you want to do and with whom?

+ What issues do you care most about? For example, you might feel strongly about gender or racial inequality or about the environment or stopping animal cruelty?

+ What values do you hold dear? For example, maybe honesty and integrity are important to you? Or perhaps justice and being treated fairly are crucial? Think about what triggers you to respond angrily or passionately as these responses often happen when our values have been stepped on, so these patterns of reaction can provide clues to what values really matter.

+ Who matters most to you?

+ What are you most grateful for about your life, as it is right now?

Once you've answered these questions you can use the information you've uncovered to look at the bigger picture of what makes you, well... you! Notice how wonderful and interesting you are! You can also use your answers to inspire you to commit to doing more of what you love with who you love and paying more attention to what matters most to you.

What's more, the better you understand what values you hold dear and the activities that spark your interest, the easier it will be to recognize those who share those values or interests and connect with people who will see you as enough, readily accept you and celebrate you for being all that you are (and veer away from those who do not).

Commit to being more authentically you

Underline the words in your answers that you want to celebrate about yourself and commit to doing and being more of, those interests and values and characteristics that make you uniquely you. When you gain the courage to be yourself, unfiltered and unapologetic, something magical happens. You begin to accept yourself more and trust your own instincts and feelings, rather than relying on external validation. When you show up as your full self, what others think matters less. This is so freeing.

Be open about your struggles and show your vulnerabilities

The truth is, none of us have our shit together, not completely. Most of us are basically winging it on a regular basis. Yet the images of perfection that we are bombarded with make us believe everyone else is doing brilliantly. Remember this is an illusion, one we contribute to each time we cover up our struggles, hide our vulnerabilities and put on a brave face. Conversely, the more open we are to sharing our struggles, the more people will relate to us and say, "Hey! Me too." This openness often has a ripple effect of realness and has the power to break down taboo subjects, just as it has begun to do with the conversation about mental health. By opening up, you can be part of the solution and find others who share the same vulnerabilities or have been through similar struggles. We're in this together, so let's keep it real.

CHAPTER THREE

The Comparison Trap

We all evaluate ourselves in reference to others. We all want what other people have. Social comparison is a natural human tendency where we compare ourselves to people who we perceive to be either doing better than us (upward comparison) or worse than us (downward comparison). This results in us "shoulding" all over ourselves, telling ourselves we should have done more, should have a better job, husband/wife/child by now. This comparative shoulding focuses on what we don't have, on what we lack. And it starts early.

From the minute we are born our families are forced into a comparison trap about our developmental achievements – how soon did we start to walk, talk and sleep through the night? At school we start to compare our abilities and grades with our peers and siblings and internalize other people's comparisons of us. As adults we compare our attractiveness, wealth, relationships, intelligence, popularity and success. Our "comparison targets" tend to be our peers, those we identify with and whose opinion matters to us, those to whom we are most similar and who have something attainable, within reach.

But with compare comes despair. Whether we "envy up" or "scorn down", a phrase coined by Princeton University psychologist Susan Fiske, comparison is a self-defeating tendency which can amplify our existing insecurities and create new ones. It can generate resentment and make us feel bad about ourselves and about those we're comparing ourselves to, which is a real shame because you're a decent human being and the person you're comparing yourself with most likely is too.

Yet comparison is probably the biggest contributor to our discontent as it can lead us to think there is something missing from our lives, even when there isn't. Comparison can dent dignity and drive, it can deflate passion and pride, and it can make you lose sight of what's right with you and lead you to focus on what you believe is wrong with you. It can make you lose track of your own unique personal value, of your own beauty, your own achievements, your own blessings. It's no wonder this leads to dissatisfaction and a sense of inadequacy in relation to those you measure yourself against.

Comparison can also stop us from stepping outside our comfort zones and taking the kind of risks which enable our personal development and growth. When you fall into the comparison trap you can end up questioning your place in life and believing that you will never be enough, do enough, have enough or feel enough. Not only is that an incredibly deflating feeling, it's also utterly untrue. And while you're comparing yourself unfavourably to other people, they're busy comparing themselves unfavourably to you. We're all caught up in this culture of constant comparison together. And even though we know compare often leads to despair, we can't seem to help ourselves.

But why? Why compare? There are two key reasons we engage in what psychologist Leon Festinger coined as "social comparison".

1. To evaluate how we are doing in relation to others.

2. To determine our place within society.

This is another evolutionary urge and survival instinct which stems from our primordial need as humans to procreate. Those who compare the most favourably within a social hierarchy would be more likely to secure the mate with the best genes, which explains why being human can sometimes feel like a competition. And we continue comparing beyond our "mating" years, because social comparison has become a habitual human tendency, a modus operandi which can be difficult to shake.

In terms of survival, it was also important for our ancestors to position themselves as an indispensable tracker or hunter, to be seen as a valued member of the tribe, someone who would not be kicked out to fend for themselves. And that need to feel valued has stuck.

According to Festinger's 1954 social comparison theory, how we stack up against others determines our self-worth. That's our actual value, how significant we are, whether or not we are good enough. So it's important to understand *why* and *how* we compare if we want to escape its entrapment and start feeling better about ourselves and valuing who we are.

Downward comparison (when we compare ourselves to those we are doing better than) can reassure us that we could be worse off and give us a boost in self-esteem to make us feel better, but it can also make us feel superior or guilty. Upward comparison can motivate us toward doing our best, but it can also make us feel inferior and inadequate.

Healthy or unhealthy comparison

These days our mobile devices give us more opportunity to fall into the comparison trap, amplifying and multiplying the number of images we see. The good news, however, is comparison doesn't have to be *all* bad. In comparing ourselves with people we admire, we can feel inspired and motivated toward self-improvement and identify our own ambitions while gaining a deeper understanding about what matters most to us.

Healthy inspirational comparison can be valuable and have a positive motivational effect on our lives. This kind of comparison offers us the opportunity to explore possibilities in the sense of "ooh, if they can do that, perhaps I can too?" Exploring possibilities, trying new activities and doing what matters most to us are good ways to spend our time. Whereas the more negative unhealthy type of comparison focuses on what we dislike about ourselves and our lives, on what we lack. So comparison can be destructive or constructive, causing desperation or inspiration. It can be a trap to fall into or a ladder to help you climb up and lift others up with you.

Understanding the difference between the two types can help us shift toward using our moments of social comparison to generate empathy with those worse off than us and to generate inspiration from those who are doing well. As long as we don't dwell on our weaknesses but learn instead to accept what we can't change and work on what we can, we can tap into this natural human tendency and use it to our advantage.

Understanding the paradox

Of course, the paradox of our lives is that we are good enough as we are and yet as humans we are also born to develop and grow, which requires learning and improvement. The key here is to remember that improving yourself doesn't mean you weren't enough before you improved. You are enough and you can improve.

If we accept that it's in our human nature to use other people as benchmarks for us to measure ourselves against, we can then decide what we do with that information, whether we use it: as a source of constructive feedback and model of what's possible, to help us improve, learn and grow, or as a source of destructive feedback and reminder of our own inadequacies, which will only keep us stuck and make us shrink.

When you consciously choose the former, you retain your power. But when you choose the latter, you give your power away – when you let how you measure up to other people determine your own self-value – you hand control over to someone else. And when you realize that what you're measuring yourself against is based on skewed data, the futility of negative social comparison becomes even more apparent.

Why negative comparison is futile

Reason 1: It's never a fair comparison

The problem is, for the most part, we are measuring ourselves against false narratives or, at least, only partial stories. So too are other people when they compare themselves to us. We are all literally comparing our real selves with partial versions of other people. Here's why: We never share our fully lived experience. Nobody does. Nor could we – none of us would have the time. We are not Truman in *The Truman Show!* We share snippets we wish to savour, magical moments on which to fondly reminisce in future, rather than the personal private dilemmas we face on a day-to-day basis.

So when we compare ourselves to people's posts on social media, we are literally comparing our blooper reel to their highlights reel, our worst bits to their best bits. Hardly a fair comparison, is it? We don't tend to post our worst selfies on social media, only the most attractive versions of ourselves and our lives are included. Then there are the extra filters which make images look even brighter and more beautiful than they really are. Everyone may look like they're having more fun, may appear to have better behaved children or a more loving partner, may seem to have more free time or greater talents, but the truth is – that's often just an illusion. Even if they have achieved more and do have certain parts of their life seemingly sorted – we never know the full story.

Think about it. What are you comparing yourself to? Social media posts? The way people appear when they're in public? The way people come across when you're in their company? When they're with you, what if you bring out the best in them and they behave quite differently behind closed doors? What if, like many of us, their house is never as neat and tidy as when people come over to visit (because they've just spent the past hour vacuuming like a person possessed)? What if they put on a brave face in public, but they're struggling in private? We might have a good cry in the shower, for instance, but don't talk about that publicly and certainly don't post on social media about it. Sometimes we might feel overwhelmed or under-appreciated, or we might have suffered loss and heartbreak, and while we may share our inner-most feelings and wrangles with our closest friends and family members from time to time, we rarely share it all – not every single detail of every single difficulty we're struggling with.

So the picture everyone gets to see of us and that we see of others is frequently far better and more polished than the reality, no matter how real and authentic we think we behave. We don't show (or know) the rest of the story. The fundamental truth is that we get and give a false impression to varying degrees because we do not and cannot share our total realities. Nor did we even before social media infiltrated our lives.

Remember the traditional photo album of old? We only included pictures of us doing exciting things, such as going on holiday and celebrating birthdays. We didn't include photos of mundane moments, like watching TV or putting the shopping away, nor the family disagreements and stressful times. The same is true today. The only difference being, back then we only shared our photo albums with a few people. Now we post our highlights more widely.

Now we all see celebratory snippets rather than the stressful struggles, which means the grass is greener on the other side because it's AstroTurf! The truth is, there are struggles behind every story, tears behind the triumphs, arguments behind the adventures, failures behind the successes.

We see the family of four standing happily at the top of the mountain they've climbed, fresh faces beaming with accomplishment, but we don't see the mother of all rows which took place in the car en route. We see the turquoise seas and sun-tanned smiles in holiday photos, but we don't see the delayed flight or the upset stomach from yesterday's seafood platter (thank goodness)! We see the beautiful twinkly eyed baby pictures, children's crafts and fun-filled adventures, but we don't see the sleep-deprived eyes of the parent or the hair-pulling moments when juggling a fussy eater and a crying baby, while having had hardly any sleep.

So how about we stop comparing our progress (or our children's) to the progress that other people appear to have made? We don't see the paths people have taken to achieve what they've achieved. We don't see every single step they've taken to get there. So how can we measure ourselves against only partial data?

The truth is, all of us are navigating our way through our own insecurities and vulnerabilities, our own issues and dilemmas, our own feelings and emotions, and we have become really good at hiding that. So we are creating mutual false impressions and then comparing ourselves to those false impressions. It makes far more sense to focus our time on creating our own path, the path which fits with our own individual experiences, strengths and knowledge.

Reason 2: There will always be someone better than you
There is always going to be someone who is more successful than you, more experienced than you and just better at certain things than you. There is always going to be someone who is prettier, slimmer, curvier, fitter, healthier than you, someone who has a bigger house, faster car, cooler hairstyle or better job than you. So if you continue to focus on what everyone else has, you'll never be satisfied with what you have,

you and your life will never be enough. And just because you notice that someone has painted a piece of art better than you or has lost more weight than you or written a better book than you, doesn't mean you should stop painting/exercising/writing. Keep going.

Reason 3: The playing field isn't always level
Some people earn achievements and success through sheer effort and determination, through making good choices and a bit of good fortune. Other people are lucky enough to have things handed to them, to be born into a privileged family background. But the latter is not always an easier path. They may not appreciate what they have as much as those who've worked hard for it. Or maybe they do and give a lot of their wealth away behind the scenes. While they may get to enjoy exotic holidays and luxury cars, they are not immune to relationship struggles, family feuds or health issues. We all face difficulties from time to time, so we should never assume people who appear to have so much actually have more than us, especially not more that matters (such as supportive relationships and the ability to appreciate what we have).

Beware the hall of mirrors
While we tend to compare ourselves to those we most relate to, we are also bombarded with media images that aren't real either. Images of celebrities and Instagram influencers are carefully curated, Photoshopped and edited. Yet we may still compare ourselves to this imagined ideal, which has been crafted to sell something to us, be it a product or a lifestyle. These images are created to impress us, and a lot of work goes into making sure that they do. But they are not real.

And even the people you consider to be the most successful or attractive have their own self-doubts and struggles, and they will compare themselves to others who have what they don't. Even celebrities can feel down when they fail to measure up to other celebrities. It doesn't matter how successful or attractive people are, we're all humans and so we all have this hardwired tendency for social comparison.

So here we all are, walking around comparing ourselves to each other's false realities in a crazy hall of mirrors, which reflect unrealistic images back to us. I say it's time to smash the glass! All of us are exactly who we are meant to be and exactly where we are meant to be. The competition and hierarchies society tells us we ought to join aren't as important to our survival as they used to be and, today, fighting to fit in and striving to be better than others tends to move us away from thriving rather than toward it. We don't need to be better than others; we simply need to appreciate where and who we are.

Reason 4: We are all unique

The only person you can truthfully compare yourself to is yourself, because only you know your full story. Siblings brought up in the same family are completely different to each other, even twins. We are all unique.

All of your own unique gifts and talents, every success and failure you've experienced, every challenge you've faced and overcome and every contribution you've made to the world are unique to you and only you. So they cannot be compared to anyone else who has their own unique lived experience. For example, there's no point comparing where you are in your life to those who were in the same year at school with you as that's where the similarities end. We've all had different experiences, lived different lives in different households, with different challenges, hardships and talents, and we've each taken different paths on our journeys. Each of us is an individual. And our individuality is our power.

There's only one thing you can absolutely guarantee being better than everyone else at and that's being you. Nobody else can be as good as you are at being you. So being yourself is literally the only competition you are guaranteed to win. So how about just being and accepting who you are, rather than letting others get in the driving seat? Of course, we know the ill-effect of comparison, yet still we do it because comparison is an intrinsic human impulse. But there's a lot we can do to mitigate the negative effects, amplify the positive and free ourselves.

STEP 8: PAUSE

One of the most important tools in our enoughness armoury is awareness. Paying attention so we can recognize when we're comparing gives us a chance to stop long enough to question it. When you notice yourself falling into the comparison trap, label the thoughts or feelings you're having. For example: disappointment, envy, judgement, scorn. Say them in your head. Labelling thoughts gives you the chance to stop them in their tracks, while labelling emotions has been proven to reduce the feelings associated with them. This technique of labelling emotions is used in mindfulness and is also employed by FBI hostage negotiators to calm situations down. Noticing, stopping and labelling gives you the opportunity to hit the pause button before you fall any deeper into the comparison trap and consider another way of looking at things.

Remind yourself that you don't know anyone's full story. The well-presented person you compare yourself to at the bus stop each morning may be in the middle of a painful divorce; the successful person who seems to do no wrong at work may have recently lost a member of their family and be struggling behind the bravado. The person who seems to achieve one accomplishment after another may be wrangling with guilt and regret. Each time you notice you are comparing yourself to others, pause and remember this.

STEP 9: TURN DESPAIR INTO POSITIVE ACTION

The despair part of "compare and despair" is amplified depending on your own situation in relation to others. For example, seeing a #soulmates post about how someone and their partner are #bestfriends can get you down if you are looking for love or in a loveless relationship. Just as #lovemyjob posts can get you down when you hate yours and dread going to work each day. If you are desperate to have children, everyone else's photographs of their seemingly perfect families may get you down and if you're a working parent who's struggling to lose weight, you'll notice all the crafty creations other parents are making with their children, along with countless slender people running marathons here, there and everywhere. In this way social media amplifies what we are lacking. But it's possible to use these comparisons to our advantage instead.

Tune in to your inner navigation system

How you feel flags up what matters most, so feelings are powerful signals in this way. Rather than ignoring those feelings or wallowing in them for too long, tune in to them and use them to make a plan. Use your feelings as a guide to what to change in your life to make you feel better. If you detest your work that much, make changing your career a priority and create an action plan based on that. Perhaps you could take evening classes or ask for training in an area you do enjoy? Or maybe you could spend one evening per week applying for jobs or volunteering for a dream employer? And if the visions of fitness are getting you down, you could persuade a friend to join you at a fun exercise class or do a 15-minute workout via YouTube every other morning. By investing time and taking action when you're comparing yourself, you can let the feelings that crop up guide you toward achieving your goals, and turn negative emotions into positive actions.

Counter the despair with feel-good activities

Some studies say that ten per cent of our thoughts are involved in comparing ourselves to others and this can result in giving up on things if they don't go to plan.[5] To counter this, commit to spending at least ten per cent of your time doing stuff you love. Immerse yourself in activities that lift you up and leave you feeling better for having done them (rather than social media scrolling, which can leave you feeling worse). Whether it's reading a good book, going swimming or attending a dance class, schedule in feel-good time to counter the times you accidentally fall into the comparison trap.

STEP 10: COMPARE ONLY AS A MOTIVATIONAL TOOL

Each of us is on our own personal development journey, all of which is unique to us and has nothing to do with how well other people are doing. As such, the only valid reason to compare is if you use it as a motivational tool so you may learn, develop and grow. There are two ways to do this:

1. Choose temporal comparison. This is different to social comparison as it involves comparing yourself against yourself. It means focusing on your own personal journey, evaluating today's progress against yesterday's and using your own past as the benchmark. Better to compare this run to your last run, rather than to those who run faster. If you are making progress (getting better at a certain skill, moving upwards in your career, getting fitter or reducing anxiety) this can spur you on without having to rely on only partial or inaccurate external data. It also makes the unequal playing field obsolete. If you are progressing, this method of measurement will motivate you to keep going. If you aren't, you can tweak your goals accordingly and celebrate smaller personal wins. And remember, just trying your best is enough.

2. Let others inspire you rather than crush you. Seek inspiration and learn from others. Read biographies, ask questions and take on wisdom from those who've walked a path before you. Just don't compare your journeys, or your beginning to their middle, as they'll have encountered different challenges and experiences to you. It's okay to have aspirations and inspirations as these can motivate us greatly and show us what is possible. Used positively, comparison can open the doors of possibility.

STEP II: APPRECIATE WHO YOU ARE AND WHERE YOU ARE NOW

Social comparison tends to focus on lack. We lose sight of our own achievements as we focus on what we haven't done and haven't got in relation to what others have. It causes us to focus on our weaknesses and inadequacies rather than our strengths and positive characteristics. So, to counter this comparison:

Find and focus on your forte

Rather than compare your weaknesses to other people's strengths, focus on your own – on your positive character traits and on what you are good at. This is the way to recognize your true value rather than relying on others to validate your worth or measuring yourself against other people. Others may admire you for these strengths but that is less important than your ability to recognize and celebrate them. In doing so you can swing that pendulum back toward the positive.

Discover your signature strengths by completing the VIA character strengths survey (www.viacharacter.org) to recognize what your character strengths are and then think about ways you can use them. We all have 24 character strengths to varying abilities. This incredibly accurate 20-minute test ranks them in order and is suitable for age ten and up. For example, my own top strengths are hope and optimism, gratitude and zest, while the top strengths of other members of my family include: leadership, love, creativity and humour. I urge you to discover what yours are. You could even create a piece of artwork featuring your top strengths and position it somewhere you can see it as a reminder. Then consider how might you deploy these superpowers of yours on a regular basis. The more you use them, the more you'll remember them when self-doubt or comparison creeps in, and the better you'll feel about yourself.

List your achievements

These need not be big race-winning, goal-achieving ones – they might include the fact you are where you are, when you could have ended up much worse off, considering what you've been through. Include small contributions you've made to the world, such as helping a friend in need or fundraising for a cause that's important to you. They could be achievements like becoming a parent and raising your child, overcoming obstacles to gain a qualification, surviving tragedies and navigating your way through grief or leaving a toxic relationship. These are all things you can be proud of. So celebrate every success and remind yourself of these from time to time.

Count your blessings

Focus on what you have instead of on what you lack. The more thankful you feel, the less you'll feel compelled to compare yourself to others. So devote time to listing all the things you have to be grateful for, and make this practice regular and habitual. You might keep a journal by your bed to record three things that you're grateful for each day, or you could start the day with a gratitude meditation or gratitude walk, running through those parts of your life that you're appreciative of.

✦ Take delight in the small everyday joys of life. Rather than wait until you hit a major milestone, feel grateful for the smaller things, from the smell of coffee as you stir your cup in the morning, to the spectacular colours of the sunset at night, from the delicious taste of the meal you've made, to the warmth of the sunshine as it falls on your face.

✦ Appreciate where you've been. You may have had a bumpy ride and have lots of regrets or bad memories from your past. You may dwell on mistakes made and challenges you've faced. But everything you've experienced has helped you to become you. Each difficulty has helped you develop and learn. So try to appreciate your past and see it as a vital part of your journey so far. And remember, it's only part of your story, which can no longer be changed. All you can do is focus on enjoying your present and looking forward to your future.

✦ Appreciate where you're going. You can't know for sure what's round the corner. The future is unpredictable but there are so many great possibilities to come. Today is just a snapshot of your life and there's so much to look forward to.

STEP 12: WE'RE IN THIS TOGETHER

We often believe everyone else is doing fine. They're not. We're not. Because we're human. And to struggle and suffer from time to time is part of being human. When we assume everyone else has it all together, we forget those other people are likely believing the same thing. We're caught up in this comparison trap together – the compare and despair feeling is mutual. So let's see that vulnerability as something that connects us all. Doing so can help us step back from the comparison trap.

To love is to stop comparing.

Bernard Grasset

Focus on our common humanity

Remember, we are all struggling to varying extents. Even those who've achieved great success and triumph have overcome obstacles to get there. And besides, none of us has every part of life sorted. Someone might have wonderful friends and have plenty to be grateful for but may be wrangling with work issues, while another person might have the strongest and most loving relationship and support of a great family but may be struggling with their health. Each of us has challenges and insecurities to deal with. When we remind ourselves of this shared human vulnerability, we can feel more empathy toward each other as imperfect humans doing our best to navigate through the uncomfortable experiences life gives us. We've been thrown together to live at the exact same time as each other so we're in this together. Let's have compassion for one another and feel connected via our human struggles.

Find joy in others' joy

Be happy for people rather than letting other people's good news make you feel bad. Instead, let other people's good news lift you up, creating a positive social contagion. When we celebrate other people's successes, we cultivate a sense of unity and pride rather than a sense of envy and disappointment.

Replace criticism with curiosity

Try to avoid judging people. It makes us disappointed in others, which rarely makes us feel good. Rather than judging other people to make yourself feel superior, which is destructive and serves nobody, stay open and accepting of others. Give people a break.

STEP 13: BE SOCIAL MEDIA SAVVY

There's not much you or I can do about the unreal imagery across social media, but we can do something about how we use it and how often. The fact we check our social feeds during our downtime – before bed, when we're queuing or commuting – means we are doing so during our most self-reflective periods, which can magnify our negative emotions.

Be aware about *how* you use social media. If you are interacting, contributing and connecting with others in a positive way, and gain a sense of mutual support through private messages and shared experiences and interests, social media can have a positive effect. But if you are passively scrolling through other people's posts and getting lost in their seemingly wonderful lives, comparing yours with theirs, you're spending less time enjoying your own life and may need to limit usage.

Have a social media detox if you feel it is having a detrimental impact. If you tend to feel frustrated, disappointed or full of doubt, then social media could be triggering a sense of inadequacy in you. So limit your social media use to weekends only or try having a week off and notice whether you feel more content as a result.

Once you reduce how much you compare and only do so sparingly as a motivational tool, you give yourself the freedom to get on with being yourself. And the more you do that, the more your definition of your own self-worth comes from inside, rather than from external sources.

When you focus your attention inward rather than outward, you realize that how good you are at being yourself is the only scorecard that matters. Once you do that, there's only one group of components left to battle – your critical committee.

CHAPTER FOUR

The Committee

"Oh, why did you have to say that? You always say the wrong thing! You should have been more thoughtful. Now she's going to think you're selfish, which she probably does already after you forgot her birthday. Remember? You're so forgetful..."

"Who do you think you are anyway? Obviously you can't do that. Don't bother trying otherwise they'll find out how awful you really are. Remember that time you tried to help Lisa with her presentation? Look how that went!" *Raises imaginary eyebrows*

"Now what are you going to do? Your customer has pressed pause on the project so you won't earn anything this month. And what if you don't get any work next month either? You'll default on the rent and then what? The landlord's bound to throw you out. You'll end up homeless at this rate!"

We all have a committee of negative self-talk inside our heads, to varying degrees (I've heard it referred to as our "shitty committee").

Committee members

There are three main committee members:

1. The brutal inner critic, who condemns, berates and judges us.

2. A doubtful imposter syndrome, which whispers in our ear about how we're not good enough and how much of a fraud we are.

3. And a negativity bias, which either focuses on the one bit of critical feedback we've been given rather than all the praise, or leaps from one worst-case scenario to the next in a spiral of doom.

The inner critic

Our inner critic is the judgemental voice that points out all the things we do wrong or badly. She (I'm going to refer to her as "she" because mine is) offers no encouragement, only scorn in the hope it might motivate us to do things better and avoid getting things wrong. In the "carrot vs stick" approach (i.e., reward vs punishment to induce behaviour), she chooses to hold a stick behind me, (the proverbial donkey) rather than dangle a carrot in front of me. But that's less effective, because motivation is about us feeling good as a result of doing something rather than feeling bad for not, so scorn and judgement tend to be less effective at motivating us to do better than praise and encouragement are. Sadly, nobody has told our inner critic that. As well as generally judging us, our inner critic also gives imposter syndrome a voice.

Imposter syndrome

Imposter syndrome can infect us all. That feeling that we don't deserve the success or job or opportunity we've been given because we're just not good enough. Michelle Obama, Emma Thompson and Tom Hanks have said they've felt this type of self-doubt, along with many celebrities, successful business people and high-profile politicians.

The term was coined in 1978 by Pauline Rose Clance and Suzanne Imes of Georgia State University, who were studying the phenomenon in high achieving women,[6] but imposter syndrome has been shown to affect men as much as women. In fact, the only people who seem immune from imposter syndrome tend to be narcissists who believe they are superior to everyone else.

The rest of us have probably experienced imposter syndrome from time to time. You know the feeling, when you're starting a new job or about to do a presentation and feelings of self-doubt suddenly envelope you. Then you think to yourself, "who do I think I am doing this when I can't even do that?" or "they'll soon find out I have no idea what I'm doing". It's like a winging-it sprite, sitting on your shoulder to remind you that, compared to everyone else here, you're clueless.

Imposter syndrome can strike with more voracity depending on the situation, so you might feel fine speaking to a group of strangers, but addressing people you know in your peer group or talking to a group of school children could turn the volume up on its put-downs. Essentially, imposter syndrome makes you feel like a fraud who is about to be found out, because it ruminates on your flaws, mistakes and lack of knowledge, rather than focusing on the effort or skills that have got you to where you are.

Your inner critic, when voicing imposter syndrome, is not focusing on your talents or hard work because, when you're in the throes of imposter syndrome, you can't internalize your accomplishments – you just think, "if only they knew" in relation to all the things you're not great at or have gotten wrong. Imposter syndrome doesn't give us permission to be an imperfect human or accept our flaws, it just bowls on in with the judgement. And, similar to when our inner critic is having a go and getting all judgemental on us, we tend to go along with it because we've been trained to, even though we know it's not helpful.

Negativity bias

The third part of our committee is our in-built negativity bias, a thought process which reacts more strongly to negative situations, comments and events than it does to positive stimuli. As psychologist Rick Hanson says, our brains are wired to "respond more intensely to unpleasant things than to equally pleasant ones. Like Velcro for negativity and Teflon for positivity". So, in a critical chorus with our inner critic and imposter syndrome, our negativity bias will focus on what might go wrong in the future and what we've done wrong in the past, rather than what might go right and what we've done well.

Why so negative and critical?

We know beating ourselves up brings us down and we may be aware of the unattributed saying that "worrying won't stop the bad stuff from happening. It just stops us from enjoying the good", so why do we criticize and chastise ourselves so much? Why do we waste so much of our time focusing on what's wrong rather than shining a light on what's right? Well, there are evolutionary and scientific reasons why our inner critic and negativity bias exist. Let me explain.

Rejection protection

Quite surprisingly, our inner critic isn't quite the bitch she (or he) appears to be. She actually has our best interests at heart. Most of the time our inner critic is actually trying to protect us from experiencing shame or embarrassment. Her primary aim is to prevent rejection, so she collects and stores negative judgements, opinions and memories and then nags us with them saying, "You *always* forget things. You *never* arrive on time. You *can't* do this! What if you fail?"

Our inner critic basically wants us to be our best selves so, when we're not, (because we're human) she gets snarky with us. She wants us to stop forgetting things, to stop being late and to stop attempting things we might fail at, because *that* would be embarrassing and lead us to be negatively perceived by others, resulting in the disapproval we fear. So our inner critic shames and blames us to protect that from happening.

You see, our inner critic is another evolutionary part of our brain that developed to *protect* us from being rejected by our fellow tribespeople, back when being an accepted and respected member of the tribe was everything. As we know, back then, if we were booted out of our tribe, we would likely not survive. As such, our inner critic is a part of our inner survival kit. She just goes about intentionally protecting us in a not-so-nice way. She's a bit harsh. Thankfully, we can reason with her. It's just a case of knowing how. (See the Inner Critic Challenge on page 71).

Primed for danger

Similarly, our in-built negativity bias may focus on the negative remarks, ignore the positive ones and dwell on what might go wrong, rather than what could go well, but in our hunter-gatherer days our negativity bias was incredibly useful.

Back then, it was better to imagine the worst than hope for the best. We were far more likely to survive if our thoughts rushed to the worst-case scenario (that we were going to get eaten by a sabre-tooth tiger), so our fight or flight response could flood our brain with adrenalin and get our body equipped and alert to deal with what we might be about to face, rather than ignore the potential threat or be optimistic about our chances, just in case.

The anxiety our negativity bias feels about what *might* happen in the future, and its ruminations about what went wrong in the past, may have muddied the enjoyment of the present but when danger was everywhere, our brains needed to be super alert and our bodies needed to be optimally primed to face that danger.

As a survival mechanism, this negativity bias prioritized pain and danger in our amygdala (our centre for emotions) above joy and pleasure, which were superfluous to our survival. Nowadays this danger of imminent death has diminished, but our negativity bias which fuels our inner critic remains.

Negativity bias is essentially the top dog of our committee because it is this focus on the fear and threat of pain and danger that drives our inner critic and imposter syndrome to speak up. Negativity bias stands at the head of the table and invites the other committee members to contribute their negative yet protective opinions to the committee meeting.

Consequently, our brains are trained to ignore or minimize praise, encouragement and compliments and instead focus on criticism, discouragement and judgements. This explains why, even if we've received praise from a large number of people, we'll end up focusing on the one piece of negative feedback we've had from one person.

I remember this happening to me after one of my Flourish workshops, (a positive psychology weekend retreat I ran for six years from 2014– 2019). I had 39 feedback forms telling me how wonderful the weekend had been and what a positive difference it had made to their attitude and so on, but one form mentioned their disappointment in staying in a grand old-fashioned hotel rather than a modern one. Guess which piece of feedback I focused on? That's all I could think about. (Luckily, I had a word with myself and was able to retune in to the lovely comments I'd had about the venue and the workshops.)

This also explains why, as Dr Robert Levenson and Dr John Gottman discovered in the 1970s, it can take as many as five positive interactions to repair one negative one.[7] So it's not our fault that we regularly feel like we're not good enough. Our shitty yet survival-based committee means well. The committee just hasn't evolved like the world has. These days we live comfortable lives compared to when our committee regularly saved us from harm.

On the upside, if you do respond well to the stick approach, as some do, your committee can feel motivational. And our negativity bias can inspire creativity and make us feel passionate enough about important causes to take action. Our negativity bias can also protect us from genuinely dangerous situations and make sure we don't step out in front of a fast-moving car or put our hand on a hot stove. However, on the whole this hardwired mental committee does us more harm mentally than good.

What this means: The preventative collaborative

Our critical commentary can stop us from trying something new that we might enjoy or prevent us from feeling brave enough to go for potentially wonderful opportunities, in case we fail. It second-guesses our gut instinct decisions and compounds the negative self-view we glean from social comparison and external feedback, further fuelling our imaginary inadequacy.

So, unfortunately, just like the pressures of perfection, the shackles of should and the comparison trap, our shitty committee can have a negative impact on how we view ourselves and show up in the world as we ruminate on past regrets, worry about the future and are prevented from enjoying our now, which sucks.

These judgemental and anxious neural processes can also lead us toward pessimism, an explanatory style we use to explain why something has happened. A pessimistic explanatory style assumes that you are always responsible for your mistakes or failures and that any success you experience is rare and just down to luck or someone else's help. So it can even stop you from enjoying your genuine achievements.

And it has all of this negative power despite many of those judgements and worries not being accurate because, when we actually look closer and investigate the vitriol and concern our negative committee members spout, we can see that much of it is untrue and cannot be justified after all. The negative self-talk coming from our committee is skewed because:

1. It's not balanced. Our negativity bias causes our minds to focus on all the things we're doing badly rather than well, so our inner critic berates us for those things, without balancing this out with encouragement for all the things we are doing right, which are far more frequent than our mistakes and failures. If you pause for a

moment and really examine your life, you'll see that you actually get a lot more right and do a lot more well than you notice. You don't notice all the things you do correctly because your brain has been designed and trained to ignore all that stuff. They become insignificant. Our mistakes and failures, however, have a spotlight shone on them because they are the dangerous things that might get us in trouble or cause rejection or disapproval.

2. It's not likely. The majority of things we worry about don't actually happen. (You can test this out too. Think about all the things you've worried about in the past that didn't come to fruition.) So even though the well-intentioned negativity bias is trying to protect you from what might go wrong, in doing so it's causing a lot of completely unnecessary worry.

3. It's not you. Although the inner critic is an internal voice, it has been created by mixing external opinions and negative memories of disapproval. So your negative self-talk doesn't originate from you at all. It is the fusion of your art teacher telling you you'd "never be a real artist with that attitude" or your parent asking, "what's wrong with you?" when you forget something again. Essentially, your inner critic is shaped by the way you've been spoken to throughout your life, by your parents, your teachers and your peers. The more discouragement, criticism and rejection you've had, and the more finger-waving suggestions that you're not good enough you've heard, the louder your negative self-talk becomes. You've simply internalized that external feedback, which, as you've repeated those thoughts often have, over time, become beliefs and mental schemas. And given that much of the external feedback and collection of criticisms comes from people who either a) only have partial data as they didn't know the full story so have made assumptions or b) really don't know you at all, much of it is, quite frankly, utter rubbish!

This third point warrants additional explanation because so much of these influencers of our inner self-worth have to do with the *external*, and the inaccuracy of external data is as dangerous to us, our mental health and our self-esteem as a sabre-tooth tiger was to our ancestors.

Dangerous data

It's problematic to shape our view of ourselves based on other people's opinions, expectations and judgements for a number of reasons. Whether people validate you by accepting and approving of you will depend on two data points:

1. the data they have about you, which is only partial, because it's likely that you've only shared part of your actual real-life experience, so they don't/can't know your whole story (even those closest to you don't live in your head)

2. the personal judgements they make as a result of their *own* lived experiences, prejudices, preferences and multiple influences – all of which have nothing to do with you. For example, they might be in a bad mood the day they criticize you or you might remind them of someone they dislike.

So when someone judges or criticizes us or seems off with us it often has nothing to do with us, and may even be inaccurate. Yet we base our sense of self-worth on it! Crazy, right?

It can even end up affecting the whole trajectory of our lives. For example, if a teacher told you your artwork wasn't good enough, this feedback might cause you to give up drawing completely and choose not to pursue a creative career. You internalize the feedback and your belief about yourself in relation to art becomes "I'm not good enough at art". But the teacher might have based that remark on how closely you followed the brief that time, rather than how good the piece was, or they might simply have been having a bad day and taken it out on you. (It happens.)

So we often end up seeing ourselves as less than we actually are based on inaccurate or partial feedback based on inaccurate or partial data! Then we internalize these distorted opinions until they become the voice of our inner critic. Damn! So what can we do about this?

STEP 14: RECOGNIZE THE GOOD, THE BAD AND THE UGLY

Firstly, we need to be able to distinguish between constructive criticism, which is well-intentioned and can motivate us to improve, and the kind of criticism that deflates us and negatively impacts how we see ourselves. It's important to recognize the difference because not being able to receive constructive criticism can get in the way of our own betterment, development and personal growth.

Now, if that art teacher had given more of an explanation, the response to her critical feedback may have been different. For example, if she'd said with greater clarity that "your artwork wasn't good enough because you haven't followed the brief this time", then added how "you're usually really good at following instructions", that "you can do better than this" and had given you a few pointers for improvement, you might have been able to take that criticism constructively and focus on curiosity rather than judgement. You might have realized you'd had a lot on your mind that day, so hadn't paid attention to the brief as well as you usually do. You could have then said to yourself, "Yeah, my artwork wasn't good enough this time, but I'll do better next time because I'll concentrate more and follow the brief".

Using this curiosity to determine whether the feedback you receive is good, bad or ugly can determine whether it motivates you to engage and persevere, which can positively impact your life (e.g., to concentrate more, get fitter, be kinder) or it has demoralized you and made you disengage and withdraw.

Consequently, the feedback we get from other people can determine whether we see ourselves as capable or incapable, as worthwhile and good enough or not. The knock-on effect of this perception then determines our behaviour. If we see ourselves as capable, we'll more likely walk into a situation feeling confident and raring to go. If we don't, our sense of inadequacy can make us less likely to want to contribute and we'll feel uncomfortable in that situation or likely to give up.

As I say in my book, *Navigating Loneliness*, as a consequence of external feedback, our self-view makes our world either feel like a positive place filled with possibilities or a difficult place filled with challenges. And it can become a self-fulfilling prophecy if we repeat these stories about our place in the world often enough. In this way, external validation can become a stumbling block, not just to how we feel about ourselves now, but also to self-improvement. Concern about what others might think and how we might be judged or rejected can stop us from making positive changes in our lives, so we stay stuck.

STEP 15: TAKE BACK CONTROL

However, if we choose instead to accept and validate ourselves, we are no longer tied to external validation and outside approval. Rather, we are free to make changes and move forward, regardless of what anyone else may think. That's not to say we ignore sound advice or constructive criticism but, once we've separated the useful feedback from the unhelpful feedback, we can make up our own minds.

What's more, once we've decided whether we want to use external feedback for our own development or reject it as unhelpful, it becomes much easier to allow and accept other people's reactions. Because we've taken back the power. Self-validation frees us from needing other people's approval. Gradually you become more willing to trust your own opinion, experiences and feelings, rather than relying on others to make you feel good about yourself. That's a great step toward feeling like you are enough. The next step is to equip yourself with the tools to talk back to your inner critic, combat imposter syndrome and counter your negativity bias.

STEP 16: REDUCE IMPOSTER SYNDROME

Remember, people who don't feel like an imposter are no more capable than you or I. It's simply that they have adjusted their thinking to believing they deserve to be where they are (because of the steps they've taken to get there). And you can too. Here's how:

✦ Talk about feeling like an imposter to others who likely feel the same. Normalize it. Knowing you are not alone in feeling like an imposter is helpful. And showing others they are not alone in feeling that way benefits them and you equally.

✦ Remind yourself why you are in your working role or why you've been invited to speak in public (or whatever situation has triggered imposter syndrome). Remember the people you are working alongside or talking to haven't invited you because of all you've done wrong, they've hired you because they've recognized all you've done right. So focus on that.

✦ See winging it as a skill rather than as proof of your position as an imposter. Everyone has to fake it until they make it from time to time, to feign confidence until they find their feet, and find your feet you will. Learning on the job is often the best way to learn, so give things time. Before long you'll gain confidence and feel more at ease, and less like an imposter.

✦ Ask yourself why you feel like an imposter in this situation? For example, it might be because you feel like an outsider. You might feel like an imposter when you are pioneering, when you are leading the way as one of the first in a minority of people to do something, yet that's an accolade worth feeling proud of, so recognize that and feel proud.

✦ Give yourself permission to be human. Other people may not know you put your underwear on back to front yesterday, left the house wearing your slippers or get flustered when you're under pressure. But you don't know all of their forgetful and flustered incidents either. Yet, the truth is, we all do these things from time to time, whether we publicly admit them or not (I put my hands up to doing all of these things).

✦ Revisit the list of all your achievements, skills and successes that you wrote down in Chapter Three and add to it if you can. Remember your strengths and efforts that have brought you to where you are. This will remind you that even if you may feel inadequate or stupid from time to time (as we all do), this doesn't mean that you are.

✦ Get yourself a strong support system of people who recognize and applaud your efforts and believe in you. The more supported you feel by those who genuinely like you for who you are, the more confidence you will have. Plus, supportive relationships have been found to be one of the most important predictors of longevity and well-being in life. And while it's important not to rely on external encouragement, a solid support network can help reduce imposter syndrome.

✦ Own your achievements. If you tend to blame yourself when things go wrong but attribute success to luck or external factors when things go right, pause to consider what parts of your life are under your control and shaped by your own choices, decisions and actions. While some events may be outside of your control, a lot will be down to your own abilities, intelligence and efforts, so own those achievements and abilities in future.

✦ Celebrate wins. Each time you achieve a goal or complete something, consider what strength or skill helped you to meet that objective and celebrate that. This is especially helpful to do if you're a parent as we all have a tendency to focus on all the evidence that suggests we are the world's worst parents. (We can't all be the world's worst, but that's what we think.) Make a note when you have a parenting win and savour it. Your mind isn't trained to notice these as much as your fails, so be prepared to do the work.

✦ Learn to receive compliments and optimize them. When you receive praise, write it down (handwrite it as this makes it more memorable) and keep a record of that positive feedback. Just like businesses collect testimonials from happy customers praising their services, if your boss or a friend gives you some praise, jot it down in a notebook or stick a note up on your wall and refer to it when you feel imposter syndrome creeping in. As well as putting a card from my friend Iva up on my wall, I've also pinned up the envelope her card came in, which says, "Thank you for being who you are". (She's awesome.) These pieces of evidence can help counter the negative feedback we give ourselves.

But what about tackling the other committee members – our inner critic and negativity bias? Thankfully, there is a field of study that can show us how.

CHAPTER FIVE

The Inner Critic Challenge

NORTH OF NEUTRAL

Positive psychology is a field which emerged in the mid-1990s. Before then, psychology focused on how to get people who were mentally unwell back to "neutral", whereas positive psychology focuses on how to get people "north of neutral". It's the science of optimal human functioning. Psychologists found that, in order to flourish, we need to deliberately notice, take in and savour the good.

Remember how our brains were designed not to remember or respond to positive stimuli as strongly as negative stimuli (at least not long enough to be converted into a proper neural structure)? Well, to reshape our brain circuitry, we literally need to balance out the negative with the positive. So that's what we're going to do now. It's time to take the Inner Critic Challenge.

Mind over chatter

New habits can take time to form but, if you can devote some time each day to working on yourself, you can master your mindset and talk back to your inner critic. In doing so you can release the hold your inner critic and negativity bias have over you. That's not to say you'll never focus on the negative again or never again give yourself a hard time – you are wired to prioritize this behaviour as a protection mechanism. But you can practise responding differently, which is where this challenge comes in.

STEP 17: NOTICE YOUR MIND CHATTER

Tune in to those Automatic Negative Thoughts (ANTs) that crop up throughout the day. Each time you hear your inner critic, imposter syndrome or negativity bias pipe up, jot down or voice record the worst judgements or most negative stories you notice.

How do you talk to yourself and what do you say? Judgemental thoughts tend to start with "They think I'm...", "I'm so...". Usually these negative judgements pop up automatically and we accept them, believe them and behave in accordance with them. But, when we stop to tune in to them, we can start to question and unpick them. This noticing part of the challenge takes practise, given the automation of these thoughts (and the busyness of our lives). Be prepared to practise regularly until it becomes habitual.

STEP 18: TAKE YOUR THOUGHTS TO COURT

Next you can begin to question the thoughts you've noted down. Disputing the critical or negative thoughts involves seeking evidence for and against them. This involves calling your inner critic to the stand and giving them a good grilling.

For example, your inner critic might say, "I always say the wrong thing". Hmmm. This can't be true because you probably say a lot of things over the space of the day and every single word you utter can't possibly be "wrong". So it's impossible that you *always* say the wrong thing. Perhaps you have a tendency to speak before thinking, but that can be worked on now you've acknowledged it. So you can throw that judgemental thought out of court too.

Let's say your inner critic has been saying "you are not worthy enough to ask for a promotion" or "you don't deserve it". You need to find evidence that will either support or deny this claim. Perhaps you feel things don't come naturally to you, you didn't get a degree in this area, and think someone else is better than you at communicating. If you failed to question these automatic judgemental thoughts, you wouldn't bother trying. But wait... there's some evidence that you *are* worthy enough. Only last week your boss praised you for your excellent work. You have been tired lately but when you apply yourself, you deliver and often exceed expectations. So, actually, there's sufficient evidence stacking up to dispute this claim and throw it out of court. Case dismissed.

Well, almost. Next you need to reframe the thought and replace it with a more accurate one. Thoughts are essentially neurons firing together to create neural pathways. These neural pathways become beliefs when they are repeated over time. This belief is that you are not good enough. To change that belief, you need to repeat thoughts that counter it, that tell you that you are, in fact, good enough after all. When we don't dispute these non-factual thoughts and stories, we default to them. And, given how many of them tend to be negative and inaccurate, this is not helpful to our well-being. Ultimately, you can either repeat inaccurate negative thoughts and be your own worst enemy or repeat more accurate positive thoughts and become your own best ally.

STEP 19: REFRAME INACCURATE THOUGHTS

Our brains are bendy. Thanks to what neuroscientists call neuroplasticity, we are able to rewire and remould our malleable minds with whatever thoughts we repeat often, so we can carve out new neural pathways and beliefs. Considering how frequently those thoughts can be inaccurate and unnecessarily cruel, the fact that we can change this will likely come as a relief. Your goal is to replace unhelpful inaccurate thoughts with more helpful and accurate ones.

So, you've grilled your inner critic in the stand and found evidence to dispute her claims. Now you can reframe each claim with a more accurate one, such as: "I am worthy enough to apply for the promotion – my boss has been impressed with my work recently and I have the skills that are needed". That sounds more accurate, so repeat those thoughts and, before long, you'll believe this to be true and apply for the job. And if you don't get the job, rather than see this as confirmation that your inner critic was right, remind yourself there are plenty of other similar roles out there which may be even better suited, and it was still a useful process to reframe your thinking and empower you to apply. You'll have learned a lot from the application process and can use the momentum to keep applying yourself to new opportunities.

STEP 20: PRACTISE REAL-TIME REFRAMING

It's not always easy to reframe thoughts as they happen, but it's a useful skill to learn. Consciously practise doing this exercise for a few days and you'll find it becomes easier. Each time you hear any negative thoughts from the committee in your mind say, "STOP". Thank the committee for trying to protect you. Explain that there's no danger here and then go through the process of taking your inner critic to court, disputing with evidence and, if there's a shred of evidence against the thoughts, reframe them. Repeat the reframed version of the original thought a few times and carry on with your day. This repetition will carve out new neural pathways and create more accurate beliefs.

STEP 21: CULTIVATE POSITIVITY WITH A NEW COMMITTEE

You can also reframe your negativity bias by focusing your attention on hearing what a more positive team of committee members might have to say. Introducing your:

✦ Inner cheerleader

✦ Joy detective

✦ Attitude of gratitude

These committee members aren't there by default. As we've learned, our brain is trained to place the other committee in power. However, with practise, they can sit on the opposite side of the table from the original committee to counter their negative impact. We'll cultivate these voices throughout the rest of this book.

Inner cheerleader

After a long day, your inner critic might reel off all the things you haven't managed to do. Meanwhile, your inner cheerleader might focus on the fact that you DID go for a long walk even if you didn't manage a run, and that you DID speak to your friend on the phone, even if you didn't drop off their card.

You only question whether you're a good enough friend, mum, daughter, sister, and so on because you care about your friend/child/parent/ sibling. The fact that you care means you are enough. Not caring would be worse. Remind yourself of that and say, "I am good enough because I care enough."

Joy detective

Your negativity bias may be focusing on why everything sucks right now. And, granted, some things may be difficult. Allow yourself to lean in to feeling those emotions – you need to feel in order to heal, so feel your frustration and disappointment, but don't dwell on them. Give yourself permission to have a brief pity party, but don't stay for too long. Start to pick yourself back up by going out into the world to find things that make you feel more hopeful, things that bring you joy. You might choose to watch the sun go down that evening or go for a walk through the woods as you know that always makes you feel better. By intentionally seeking out moments of joy, you can counter the negative and pay some positive emotion into your positivity bank account.

Attitude of gratitude

Your negativity bias may be focusing on all the things that have gone wrong today. Perhaps you dropped your phone in the toilet, got the time wrong for an important call and/or spilt coffee on your laptop. Maybe a family member has upset you or you're feeling overwhelmed with work. All of this can bring you down but, if you look for it, there will be something to be grateful for. You were able to mop up the coffee in time to avoid a keyboard malfunction, you have fresh water and technology at your disposal, you have members of your family available for a hug and you have work. There is always something to be grateful for, whether you look on the bright side of a bad situation or mentally list all the things that were good about your day and are good about your life.

Your inner cheerleader, joy detective and attitude of gratitude are the silver lining to the cloud cast by your inner critic, imposter syndrome and negativity bias. And they need to be nurtured. It's time to give this new positive committee the stand.

✦ Create a smile file – either on your computer, on your phone or, if you're more of an analogue person than a digital one, in a scrapbook or notebook. List all the things your inner cheerleader would say about you – all the encouragement and praise you've received. Make a list of everything you've achieved, from winning a medal at school or doing a drawing you were really proud of, to securing a job you'd applied for or completing a running course. Also list everything you've coped with or endured in your life, be it loss, lack of opportunity or other adversities and hardships.

✦ Keep a gratitude journal and/or gratitude photo album to record what you are grateful for a few times a week. Don't make it a chore, just add to it as often as you can, and not just on good days. Try to write down (or take photos of) a few things you're grateful for on days which haven't gone so well, to practise finding that silver lining in every cloud and giving your attitude of gratitude committee member a strong voice. Flick through this whenever you're feeling a bit glum.

✦ Spend a morning or afternoon performing random acts of kindness and notice how much positive emotion floods your body. From delivering daffodils to friends, to sellotaping a few pound coins on a parking meter and donating clothes to charity – positive psychologists have found, along with practising gratitude, that kindness is one of the most feel-good interventions there is. It will wrap you in what's called "giver's glow" and make you feel as good as the recipient of your kindness.

By giving yourself the tools and opportunity to counter negative self-talk with something more positive, you can redress the imbalance that all of these external and internal influences can have over your life. And, when it comes to feeling good about yourself, balance is everything.

PART TWO

GOOD ENOUGH –
THE IMPORTANCE
OF BALANCE

Until you stop breathing, there's more right with you than wrong with you.

Jon Kabat-Zinn

We can't control what other people think of us, only what *we* think and how *we* feel about ourselves. In Part One, we explored how our own self-view can be impacted significantly by external input and what we can do to counter this.

Now, it's time to focus on finding that happy medium. To find that sense of balance that enables us to be enough, have enough, do enough, look enough and feel enough.

CHAPTER SIX

Being Enough

Being enough, I think, is about three things:

- ✦ feeling good enough about being human.

- ✦ feeling good enough about who we are as individuals.

- ✦ valuing ourselves enough to believe we are worthy of love, belonging and success in life (whatever that may look like to us).

Being human

Feeling good enough about being human means showing up as best we can on any given day, but also knowing that some days we may falter – and accepting that.

It's about writing ourselves a permission slip to be human, which means accepting that sometimes being human will feel messy, sometimes we'll get angry and shout, or cry or forget or stumble. We might misunderstand or be misunderstood. We might say or do something we really wish we hadn't, especially when we're tired or hungry (I'm looking at you, "hangry") and, sometimes, we might not show up in the world as we'd hoped, but we can accept all of this as simply part of what it means to be human and real.

Feeling good enough about being human is about accepting who we are, warts and all. It's about feeling like we are good enough not *despite* making mistakes or when life feels particularly hard but *because* we've made mistakes and *because* we're navigating our way through tough times. It's this sense of knowing that is how life is as it's meant to be – a sometimes scary rollercoaster of ups and downs – and that living a good enough life is simply about strapping ourselves in to ride that rollercoaster.

Feeling good enough about being human is like a solid hand gently squeezing our shoulder to say, "you are enough, things may not be okay right now in this moment, but they can and will be again". It's about acknowledging and accepting that screwing up is part of life, so it's natural and human and therefore good enough.

Self-approval

Feeling good enough about who we are is important because of what can happen when we don't. When you slip into this belief that you are not a good enough person, you can fall into the habit of operating from this place of deficiency and inadequacy, which can have a damaging knock-on effect of becoming a self-fulfilling prophecy.

Our performance tends to align with how we see ourselves, so how we think can affect our results. When you think "I'm terrible at this" you don't try to do it, so you don't get better at it and you *stay* terrible at it. Either that or your self-doubt causes you to make more mistakes than you would ordinarily, which negatively impacts your performance. That process only serves to prove your self-doubt right, giving you more evidence to question your adequacy and disapprove of yourself. This creates a loop of insufficiency and it's not helpful.

Believing you are not enough is an insult to your utter fabulousness and prevents you from living the kind of life that *will* feel good enough to you. That insulting belief just gets in your way. Conversely, when you approve of yourself, you can notice the situations which trigger you to feel like you're not enough for what they are – individual moments or experiences which you can learn from and which don't make you inadequate.

Self-approval involves finding enough evidence to support the fact that you are good enough to counter the evidence that says you are not. It's about giving your inner cheerleader a voice that is loud enough to shush your inner critic. It's about acknowledging that much of the negative self-talk is inaccurate, misjudged and not flexible enough to be true.

Feeling good enough about who you are as an individual is about acknowledging and celebrating what you do right and what's right with you, while accepting that there will always be room for growth and improvement, and that you will always be an unfinished, yet incredibly beautiful, piece of art that is constantly a work in progress.

Self-worth

Valuing ourselves enough means seeing the value in that piece of art that is us, to consider ourselves valuable and worthy enough to invest time and effort into improving whatever we wish to improve, so we can show up as best we can be but without those pressuring "shoulds". Knowing you are a perpetual work in progress keeps you open to learning and accepting those parts of you that you cannot or needn't change, because you're good enough as you are.

When we see ourselves through this lens of self-approval, we are better able to enjoy the journey because we can better balance who we already are with who we hope to become. Whereas the less we value ourselves, the less power we give ourselves.

Having self-worth is about choosing to stop letting external factors influence how deserving you believe you are. It's about choosing instead to SEE YOUR WORTH and RECOGNIZE YOUR VALUE! Your worth is inherent – you were valuable and worthy when you came into the world and you've only improved since then. No matter what anyone else thinks of you now or thought of you then, you were an incredible miracle when you were born and, as you've grown, you've become more so. Isn't it about time you noticed that?

Repeat after me:

I am worthy of love and respect.

I am unique and that makes me awesome.

I am a valuable human being!

These words may not feel natural for you yet but that's okay.

Just right

The status quo for most of us is we tend to think that we are either too much this or not enough that (thanks to internalizing external opinion and expectation).

What do you think you are *too much* of? For example: too sensitive, too judgemental, too trusting, too loud, too quiet?

What do you think you are *not enough* of? For example: not kind, trusting, confident, calm enough?

Isn't it interesting that you've decided there is a perfect "enoughness" of sensitivity, loudness, quietness, confidence or calm, as if there is a spirit level measuring whether you are too much or too little, rather than just right. Yet, you are you, which means you are already just right as you are – this is how you are meant to be – perfectly imperfect.

Sure, maybe you could work on your kindness, confidence or patience, or qualities you think will genuinely help you get where you want to be in life, and that gentle growth is part of living, but you are still good enough. So it's time to bring the balance back.

STEP 22: BE YOURSELF AND BALANCE SELF-IMPROVEMENT WITH SELF-APPROVAL

We've been conditioned to think we need to be the absolute best we can be. But being our best consistently is not realistic or sustainable, nor is it human. And is life really about being our best selves or is it more about just being *ourselves*? Sometimes being our "best selves" may come at the expense of being authentic as we do what is expected of us, rather than what feels right to us.

What if, instead, we saw our job as human beings on this planet to be as *us* as we can be? So, rather than constantly feeling under pressure to improve and do better and be the best, what if you just needed to be as YOU as you can? To simply become who you truly are and to know yourself well enough to understand who that is. So, what if, on waking, instead of saying, "Today, I'm going to get this and that done, I'm going to achieve this goal and I'm going to be the best version of myself," you gave yourself a more achievable objective and said, "Today, I'm going to be the me-est me I can be." How would that feel? More achievable, right?

This is not to say you stop putting in effort to achieve things you hope to. Nor does it mean you should stop setting goals or give up on the whole notion of self-improvement. As human beings we need to feel like we're growing, progressing and doing our best to live meaningful lives. Accomplishment is one of the "pillars of well-being" according to the positive psychology researchers who have defined the foundations of how we can optimally function and flourish.[8]

But, when the pressure to achieve, strive and improve gets on top of us and squishes us down, that's when it can become problematic. To be our authentic selves, it's all about balance, because to find the happy medium we need to balance our desire and commitment for self-improvement with the approval of ourselves as we already are. There are a number of ways we can find this balance.

YOU enough

Rather than questioning if you're good enough, ask yourself, are you being YOU enough? The simple reframing of this question gives you permission to be all that you are – a mixture of strengths and weaknesses, admirable traits and less desirable but equally authentic flaws. Being the you-est you will involve making mistakes and messing up occasionally. Expect this and accept it, because it's normal.

Are you acting with integrity? Sometimes, when we do or say something that goes against our values or that just doesn't feel right, it means we've behaved in a way that isn't authentic, and that can make us feel like we're not being ourselves. Revisit page 38 to remind yourself of your values and come up with a bunch of ways you can live your values and be more you on a daily basis. For example, perhaps you tend to go along with conversations that you don't feel comfortable participating in because you don't want to rock the boat, but perhaps it would feel more authentic to change the subject or leave the room to get a drink?

Reframe the notion of being yourself as brave rather than embarrassing. See and celebrate the courage it takes to be yourself with all your quirks and imperfections. Being 100 per cent you is a more natural way to be, but, thanks to our conditioning, it can take some practise to let go, be vulnerable and true.

Value your individuality – nobody else looks, thinks or behaves exactly like you. Even identical twins and triplets have differences, be they opinions, mannerisms or musical preferences. You are a unique human being among almost eight billion people, with a different set of fingerprints and your own individual way of being. That in itself makes you very special and awesome and who you were born to be.

Prioritize self-improvement based on your values and act upon them. Revisit the answers to the quiz you took in Chapter Two to align improvements with what matters most to you. For example, if being a good friend/parent/sibling is a top priority, you might decide to work on your listening skills. Or, if being kind is a value of yours, you might wish to develop your kindness by spending a morning or afternoon performing random acts of kindness and seeing how much positive emotion floods your body.

Work on improving what you can and want to change. Consider your weaknesses or flaws, the parts of you that your inner critic tends to focus on – those parts which, if you had a magic wand, you would consider changing. It could be a lack of patience, artistic talent or cooking ability. These observations about what's missing or lacking generally fall into two categories – things you could change or improve and things you can't. For example, you can learn how to develop your artistic talent and cooking skills, you could even try to improve your patience by reading books or watching videos on the subject. Before investing time or money into improving any of these things though, make sure they are what YOU want rather than what society says you *should* want. If it's the latter, let them go. If you really want to make improvements, choose one thing at a time to work on improving and create an action plan to help. Then feel good about yourself for taking devoted action, no matter how small, to personally develop and grow.

STEP 23: BALANCE CELEBRATING STRENGTHS WITH ACCEPTING WEAKNESSES

Here is a list of more negative feedback I've received from other people over the years, which has fed into my own inner critic:

- ✦ I'm too sensitive, messy, scruffy, dizzy, forgetful, independent and keen.

- ✦ I overthink things, apologize too much, care too much about what's going on in the world, rather than what's going on closer to home.

- ✦ I'm not tidy, slim, tall or fit enough, my boobs aren't big enough, my hair is not sleek enough, my posture is not straight enough and my teeth are not white enough.

Well, f*&% THAT!

To quote Gloria Gaynor, "I am what I am." Humble modesty is fine but what about saying, "I value myself", "I am worthy", "I am who I am unapologetically, regardless of anyone else's approval or disapproval" and "I approve of myself!" Being me is about being and accepting *all* of those perceived flaws along with the more positive parts that make me who I am. This kind of acceptance helps you to sustain a secure sense of self, feel good about yourself and recognize your own value regardless of external feedback.

Revisit the VIA character strengths and other strengths you uncovered in Step 11 and during the self-quiz. These may not actually feel like strengths to you because they come naturally to you, but that's why they are your superpowers – your own strengths don't come naturally to everyone. We each have different superpowers. Each time you feel yourself feeling a bit down about whether you are being enough of a good human, whip out your list and read through it as a reminder that you are enough.

Develop your inner cheerleader

You know yourself better than anyone else knows you, so what if you only ever saw the best in you? Sounds like a foreign concept, right? Like when someone compliments you – "Oh, you're so good at that – you're such an inspiration." You're like, "Wait, what? Me?" Looking around to check they're actually referring to you and not the person stood behind you.

What if you saw yourself through the eyes of someone who believes in you, someone who admires you and sees your potential and possibilities? What if you saw yourself through the eyes of an adoring baby, marvelling at your brilliance as they look up at you full of wonder and admiration? Yes, be your own friend, but be your own FAN too!

Seeing yourself as not good enough is like a sunset thinking it's not orange enough or too glowy, or a mountain thinking it's not high enough or too jaggedy. The sunset is amazing, the mountain is amazing, YOU are amazing! Remind yourself of that often by seeing the best in yourself.

See yourself as deserving and be your own encourager

This is important because, when you believe you don't deserve something, it becomes difficult to attract that something into your life. Your energy determines your request.

Write down the following: "I deserve to feel good about myself because..." then fill in the gaps. "I deserve to achieve my dreams because..." then fill in the gaps. For example: "because I'm unique and have more good in me than bad" or "because I work hard and try my best and, quite frankly, I'm a bloody nice person."

It's natural to feel demoralized and not good enough when we don't receive the praise we feel we deserve. However, the lack of positive feedback usually has nothing to do with us. The prospective encourager may be too busy to offer feedback or might struggle with articulating praise. So give yourself a pat on the back rather than wait for it from others.

By finding a sense of balance between working on parts of yourself that you wish to improve and accepting parts of yourself as good enough, you can see that you *are* being enough. By devoting more time to focusing on your strengths and less time dwelling on your weaknesses, you can bring the balance back to a happier medium of enoughness.

CHAPTER SEVEN

Having Enough

Being at peace with who you are is one part of enoughness. Being at peace with what you have is another. Unfortunately, it's common for those of us living in the Western world to focus on what we *don't* have rather than on what we *do* have. We often ignore the abundance we have in our lives – be that love, health, support, friends, and so on – and focus instead on what we don't have enough of – be that money, time, energy, clothes, opportunities, social media likes, and so forth.

We take for granted what we already have – eyes that get to see the blue sky, rainbows and the faces of loved ones; ears to hear birdsong, music, raindrops and laughter. We have senses that enable us to feel the coolness of grass on bare feet, to smell coffee and flowers and bread being baked, to taste chocolate and oranges and hot cups of tea. But we focus on what we don't yet have – a flatter stomach, bigger house, faster car, cooler clothes.

We might have a great deal to be grateful for – a few solid friendships, a loving family, maybe even a job we quite enjoy and our health, but if we don't get the best grades, look like an air-brushed Amazonian goddess and earn enough to buy an amazing house, well that's just not good enough, or so we're told.

Being satisfied enough with life means finding that happy medium between striving for what you wish to have and appreciating what you already have. Achieving such balance between aspiration and appreciation can greatly impact levels of life satisfaction.

Be content with what you have; rejoice in the way things are. When you realize there is nothing lacking, the whole world belongs to you.

Lao Tzu

The added bonus of developing your attitude of gratitude by focusing attention on appreciation and counting your blessings (which soon add up) is that you begin to notice abundance more often than you notice scarcity. And when that happens, you soon realize you already have (more than) enough. When you focus on being thankful for what you already have, you see the world from a place of plenty.

Adaptation and the hedonic treadmill

Of course, us humans being the complex folk we are, boosting life satisfaction to "good enough" levels is not quite as simple as remembering to count your blessings. There's another mind-trick we need to navigate first to combat the sense that we don't have enough and consequently want more.

Just as we've seen throughout this book, there is a scientific reason why we think and behave in the ways we do. And this sense of constantly wanting more is another example of how the human mind works. We say, "I'll be happy/happier when..." followed by whatever we wish for. For example, "...I get that promotion", "...I have a child", "...I have a bigger garden", "...I travel the world", and so on.

The problem is the "I'll be happy when..." arrival fallacy simply postpones satisfaction in lieu of achievement or material gain, especially given how quickly the novelty wears off, once we've grown accustomed to what we've achieved or bought. For, just as our lowest lows don't last, nor do our highest highs. We habituate to them, adjusting quickly to both positive and negative events and returning to the same level of satisfaction we enjoyed before we experienced the fleeting feeling of pleasure.

This ability to adjust to our circumstances is called "adaptation" and it keeps us on what psychologists call "the hedonic treadmill" – a perpetual loop of trading up and achieving, or buying more and experiencing pleasure, which soon fades, causing us to desire more, and on and on it goes, because we'll always need more. This is the "more war" that can lead to never feeling like we have enough of what we think we need to be happy.

Additionally, according to the economic "law of diminishing marginal utility" devised by German economist Hermann Heinrich Gossen in 1854,[9] the more we have of something, the less happiness we gain from it. This, combined with our adaptation to material gains, explains why externalities – such as the next toy or achievement, or windfall or promotion – do not boost our happiness for long.

It also explains why even lottery winners find themselves returning to the previous level of satisfaction soon after their life-changing windfall. Novelty wears off. Now this may sound rather depressing in a "what's the point of striving if none of it makes you happy for long" kind of way, but that's where the importance of balance comes in to play.

Balancing ambition with appreciation

Accomplishing more is about progress and growth and that's an important part of life, so the fact we adapt doesn't mean we should avoid setting goals altogether. Rather, if we balance our ambition to succeed in the future with our appreciation for what we already have, we can maintain a stronger sense of well-being for longer and feel like we have enough.

What's more, we can use this knowledge to our advantage. Knowing that accumulating more only brings temporary satisfaction can have a positive effect as it can make us appreciate and savour these moments more deeply, aware that they are only fleeting, and therefore see the sense in developing our attitude of gratitude and joy detective committee members. It can also help us ensure that we put our efforts into gaining and achieving what we really want (rather than what other people and society want for us). As such, there are many ways we can win this "more war", step off the hedonic treadmill and bring balance to our levels of life satisfaction.

STEP 24: BALANCE GRATITUDE AND GROWTH

Striving can have both a positive and negative effect on us. The dissatisfaction caused by feeling like you're not successful or happy or thin or young enough can make you feel like you've failed and are therefore less than enough.

However, sometimes dissatisfaction is useful and can provide the impetus to make a change and get things done. Great things can come from dissatisfaction if you use it to motivate you, and the resulting efforts can make a real difference.

What's more, it's possible to offset our natural adaptation to the novel by creating an environment that balances gratitude with growth, by focusing equal attention on what we have now, rather than focusing predominantly on what we hope to have in the future. Because none of our achievements mean anything if we're not content in the moment.

So on one hand, it's important to have a clear vision of what you'd like to accomplish during your lifetime, as this will spur you forward to grow. On the other hand, it's important to value how far you've already come. It's time for your inner cheerleader and attitude of gratitude to work together.

✦ Write a gratitude list. There are different ways to record gratitude. During the Inner Critic Challenge (on page 75) you created a smile file and gratitude journal/photo album to record what you are grateful for each day, to counter negativity. This time, jot down a list of things you appreciate about how your life is more generally. For example, the fact that you are healthy, you have strong friendships, perhaps the fact that you have a job and can put food on the table, or the fact that your sibling lives nearby (or far away, depending on your relationship).

✦ Regularly practise developing your attitude of gratitude, especially during moments of frustration or dissatisfaction. Stop yourself and say, "I wonder what a different way of looking at this might be?" For example, you might be thinking, "this job sucks" or "he never tells me he loves me" or "my family can be so annoying!" But there must be one good thing, so try shifting your attention toward that. Perhaps, "this job can be dull, but I do like working with these people." Or "he doesn't tell me he loves me, but he does *show* me each time he fills the car up with fuel or brings in the washing when he knows I'm busy" or "I'm grateful my family is healthy." Finding something to be grateful for during testing times is great practice.

✦ Write a growth list. Jot down some growth goals – things you'd like to achieve or improve upon. For example, they might include wanting to cultivate a regular meditation practice or complete a Couch to 5K running challenge. Enlist your inner cheerleader to remind yourself that you can do these.

✦ Consider the motivation behind your goals. What would achieving these goals give you? A feeling of security and comfort? The ability to impress family and friends? Pride and confidence in yourself and your abilities? Your motivation shapes why this goal is so important to you, but also gives you a plan B. If you are unable to achieve your goal, rather than feel like you haven't achieved enough, there may be other ways to create the same feelings. For instance, if your goal is to save for a deposit on your dream home and your "why" is to give you those feelings of security, pride and confidence in yourself, by listing other ways you can feel those feelings right now (such as joining a community group, moving your furniture around to feel more homely, stocking up on candles and cushions to create a more comforting space) you can enjoy the journey and experience similar feelings that attainment of your goal would provide.

✦ Pave the way for change. Just as dissatisfaction can be a useful catalyst for creating necessary changes in the wider world, if it's combined with a sense of hope, it can also act as a catalyst to inspire changes in your life. So if you find yourself feeling dissatisfied quite regularly, think about what is creating this feeling and what you can do about it, pro-actively, to change the situation causing it. Make a list of tiny steps you could make to lift yourself out of circumstances that are causing these feelings of dissatisfaction, then act on them. This activity will make you feel like you are doing enough to navigate your way toward something better. And your hope will encourage you to keep going.

When our intentions come from a place of contentment or hope, they have far more power than when they come from a place of lack. Thriving with intention always trumps striving in desperation. Hence the importance of cultivating gratitude in our lives as a foundation from which to dream.

STEP 25: ENJOY THE JOURNEY

Striving to achieve things only becomes problematic if we stop enjoying the journey toward our destination. If your fixation on future gratification reduces your pleasure within the present – if you find yourself focusing so intently on the end result that you forget to cherish your current contentment – it's time to redress the balance.

Gardeners don't wait until every flower is in full bloom to enjoy their gardens. They delight in each new bud and cherish the time they spend tending to each blossom, step-by-step. Similarly, we shouldn't wait until we've achieved our goals to enjoy our lives. Instead, let's delight in each small step we take toward bringing our goals to fruition, for each little action has meaning and significance and is worth celebrating immediately.

✦ Stop to smell the roses – savour and cherish your current reality. Savouring is a vital part of gratitude, as it helps us carve out positive memories that stay with us. "The problem with positive thinking is that it sometimes just stays up 'in the head' and fails to drip down to become a fully embodied experience," says psychology professor Barbara Fredrickson. To fully relish your reality, experts suggest that you focus your attention on your feelings of appreciation for as long as you can (at least ten seconds) and let those feelings sink deep into your body. Notice where in your body you feel that emotion. How does it feel? Savouring in this way instils the positive experience into your memory bank, while also giving your current well-being a healthy boost.

✦ Practise being mindful. Gratitude is about focusing our attention on what we have now. Mindfulness is about focusing our attention on what we are experiencing now. Mindfulness enables us to slip from automatic into manual, so we can fully see and experience each moment with delight and wonder. To start your own mindfulness practice, tune in to your senses and notice what you can see as you look around you, what you can hear as you listen intently, what you can feel as you notice how your clothes feel against your skin or how your feet feel against the ground, what you can smell as you focus on the scents around you and try to describe them and on what you can taste. Another way to practise mindfulness is to practise a mindful breathing meditation, which is simply about focusing your attention on your breath as you inhale and exhale, and each time your mind wanders, which it will, just gently bring your attention back to your breath, over and over again.

✦ Enjoy the process. Focus on enjoying the small steps and actions taken and seeing the value in them. Shift your mindset to focus on the journey rather than the destination. Shift "I'll be happier when..." to "I'm happy to have the opportunity to try, to take this step forward." Viewing the process of growth and achievement as being equally rewarding as the reward itself helps you see your satisfaction (i.e., the general feeling of enoughness) as a by-product of the process, rather than as a destination or goal in itself. Otherwise, once you've arrived at this destination of feeling like you have enough and have achieved enough, what's next? Valuing the process rather than the product, the journey rather than the destination, gives us the chance to step off the hedonic treadmill and enjoy now.

✦ Enjoy your progress. Don't wait until the end to reward yourself, celebrate little wins along the way. Treat yourself just for progressing. Whether you were able to help someone out, make someone smile or write a few paragraphs of a blog post, celebrate heading in the right direction. If your goal is to meditate/exercise/sleep/contribute to your community/see friends more – a few minutes more is enough because that's progress, and all progress is growth. Even slow progress is still progress.

STEP 26: CHOOSE EXPERIENCES OVER STUFF

Conspicuous consumption (our desire to keep up with the Joneses, which stems from that in-built social comparison) is partially responsible for fuelling our desire for more and preventing us from stepping off the treadmill. But, as author Dave Ramsey says, "We are spending money we don't have to buy stuff we don't need to impress people we don't like." Perhaps realizing we don't need to accumulate so much stuff is sufficient treasure?

According to psychology professors at Cornell University, happy memories we gain from experiences last much longer than the pleasure we gain from purchasing things.[10] They discovered that people's satisfaction with the items they bought went down over time, whereas their satisfaction with experiences they had bought rose over time.

This is because experiences enable us to connect with those who were involved in them, or who have undergone something similar. Furthermore, experiences evoke memories. We are better able to internalize experiences than objects. So experiences become a part of us and create fond memories that we are able to store and access, reminding us that we are living good enough lives.

✦ Buy experiences rather than just things: Ideally look for experiences that involve others and are a long-way off, so you can enjoy the anticipation of the event, savour the experience itself as it happens, then reminisce on your memory of the event as time passes – a wonderful way to amplify and enhance the pleasure of a single purchase. Experiences don't have to cost the earth either – there's lots of free fun available: a woodland treasure hunt with friends and family, a cup of hot chocolate around a campfire, wild swimming in a local lake or river, family bike rides and picnics.

✦ Do something right now that you love to do. Remember, success isn't always about achieving something in the future – it can be about enjoying something that you love in this moment. That's success enough. So try to do more of what matters most to you. If you need a reminder of what that is, make a bookmark or write on a sticky note the things that light you up (revisit the self-interview on page 37) – for example, reading poetry, having a soak in the bath, having a squeezy hug, sitting still near water and listening to the sounds of nature.

Having enough isn't just about having possessions or achievements, it's about having fun and balancing ambition with appreciation. Finding that happy medium allows you to enjoy now and feel satisfied that you have enough in the moment.

CHAPTER EIGHT

Doing Enough

"How are you?" friends ask. "Good thanks, just so busy! It's manic," we reply. And it is. Feeling like we're doing enough isn't easy in today's always-on 24/7 world where every moment seems to be filled. We increasingly wear our busyness as a badge of honour, as validation and proof that we must be doing okay and meeting expectations, or as an excuse for why we can't squeeze everything in. Just. So. Busy!

It's easy to get so wrapped up in our daily doings that we forget to just be. This buzz of busyness is constant as we're distracted by deadlines and noisy phone notifications; priorities, productivity and achievement have overridden serenity and contentment. Always "doing" has replaced the space where just "being" once lived.

Our never-ending to-do lists suggest that we're not doing enough, that there's simply "not enough time in the day" to do everything we need to do, even when we've done plenty. As such, it's easy to operate from a place of lack, where time is seen as scarce.

There are three ways to combat this sense of time scarcity and move toward a sense of having enough time and doing enough with it:

1. Plan and prioritize

2. Pause often

3. Balance doing with being

STEP 27: PLAN AND PRIORITIZE

Feeling like we don't have enough time or that we haven't done enough can create stress and overwhelm. But with a little effort and planning, we can gain more control over how we spend our time and make the most of it. The juggle may be real but there are ways to optimize our time.

✦ Synergize your time. Which activities could you fit into the same time block? Let's say your to-do list includes the following tasks: walking the dog, making a delivery and checking in on a friend. That's three tasks you could fit into one hour if you invite your friend on your dog walk to wherever you need to make a delivery and talk as you walk? Or perhaps you could have a batch cooking party with friends to make a variety of meals ready for the week ahead, having caught up with people in the process. Or maybe you want to do more exercise and see more of a sibling. Perhaps you could set up a Sunday morning family cycle ride as a weekly event?

✦ Set up routines. The more certainty and clarity we have over our everyday routine, the calmer life can be because we've automated our decisions. We no longer need to decide whether to go to the gym or who will collect so and so from such and such, because it's already a fixed routine. Routines can also help us focus and minimize distraction. If part of our routine is to reply to emails and messages in the final half-hour of our working day, we can turn off notifications knowing we'll respond during an already allocated time period.

✦ Prioritize the basics to optimize energy. We need a balanced diet of the four cornerstones of vitality: nutritious food, plenty of water, sufficient movement and sleep to nourish us. Vitality is one of the main pillars of well-being and helps our minds and bodies to function optimally. So put these atop your to-do list.

STEP 28: PAUSE OFTEN

Striving can be tiring so it's okay to give yourself time off. Remind yourself that without sufficient self-care or downtime you'll be less productive and alert, so giving yourself time to pause is an investment in working optimally. The more we cram in to our days, the more overwhelmed and under-pressure we feel and the less able we are to function at our best. Essentially (and ironically) we tend to get more done (and done well) the more breaks we give ourselves. It's easier to focus and get in to tasks and projects if we feel nourished, so donating some of our precious time to having regular breaks is especially important the higher our plates are piled. Odd as it sounds, if you want to do more, do less. Or at least, find the right balance between high energy periods (where you plough through tasks and accomplish a lot) with low energy downtime (where you take a break, slow down and look up).

✦ Enforce the pause. Reward each "power hour" of focused hard work with a break. Set an alarm to go off each hour where you pause for a few minutes, look around you, take a few deep breaths or put the radio on and have a quick boogie.

✦ Plan your week to include downtime. Even 15-minute periods of rest can work wonders and help you process and come up with fresh ideas. For example, you could take a walk round the block to clear your head and get some fresh air, pause to look out the window and try to notice something new or simply get a drink of water and tune in to your senses as you slowly sip it.

✦ Get rid of lengthy to-do lists. Commit to doing three things each day to help you achieve your goals or things that simply need to be done – these can be big or small. Completing those three tasks means you are doing enough. Anything else is a bonus.

✦ Meditate. In between big tasks or first thing in the morning, focus on your breathing. It only takes a moment to ground yourself. So, set your timer for five minutes and focus on counting your inhale in for four, hold for four, exhale for four, hold for four. Repeat this "box breathing" and, each time you feel your mind wandering, bring your attention back to your breath as this enables you to home in on the present moment.

STEP 29: BALANCE DOING WITH BEING

Part of the everyday strife of modern life seems to be this tension between feeling obliged to make the most of each day and being relaxed and content with ordinary, yet good-enough living. The remedy here is finding balance between *doing* and *being* so you can welcome and accept the possibility that you've done enough of both.

Cultivate lagom

The Swedish tradition of *lagom* is centred around balance. Translated, it means "not too little, not too much, just right". And, given the temporary nature of material pleasures (as we've seen from the hedonic treadmill) it's a wise concept to follow, as it seeks out a happy medium between decadence and deficiency and between productivity and stillness, toward a balanced life.

- Check in once a month to assess your work-life balance. If you are working so hard you don't have enough time for you, what can you do about this?

- Take leisurely strolls in nature as part of your lunch break. Time outdoors has been shown to boost creativity and productivity so it's time well spent. You'll return to your workplace feeling refreshed and ready to go and you'll likely come up with new ideas you may not have had without that fresh air. Outdoor walking meetings are a good way to balance the need for fresh air and exercise with the need to discuss important work issues with colleagues or clients too.

- Put things off. Unless something drastic happens, there is always tomorrow. Most things can wait. Even deadlines can have some flexibility. So before ploughing ahead with tasks, ask yourself whether the deadline is imperative and whether it will be detrimental if you save that task until tomorrow?

- Balance social gatherings with alone time. The Swedish concept of *fika* ("a break from doing") enables Swedes to prioritize their work–life balance, including social gatherings over coffee and "me-time". It's important to balance these too, so you don't feel over-committed and get the chance to process your days, by spending some of your time in solitude.

Balance enjoyment with responsibility

Do what you love to do rather than what you think you should do as often as you can. When you spend all of your time doing what you should rather than what you'd like to be doing, you can feel frustrated, disappointed and dissatisfied. We all have responsibilities and may have tasks we'd rather not have to do, but if we can balance that with doing what we absolutely love, we can gain that happy medium between pleasure and responsibility.

Choose activities which offer "flow" experiences

Flow is when you are so immersed and absorbed by an activity that you lose track of time. This kind of engagement is important to well-being and to our overall feeling of life satisfaction. According to psychologist Mihaly Csikszentmihalyi, flow-inducing activities are the kind that are sufficiently challenging to enable improvement and sustain interest, but not so challenging that enjoyment in the activity is lost. For example, painting using a new but doable technique, or playing a piece of music you can master but that will take some effort. Invest time in hobbies that offer this balance.

Swap "having a purpose" with "being purposeful"

There's a lot of pressure on us nowadays to ensure we are living with purpose and contributing in some way. But if we reframe purpose as a verb, it's easier to find opportunities to do something purposeful. For example, rather than only feeling like you've done enough if you achieve your dream of becoming a teacher/writer/mother/entertainer, you can seek opportunities to teach, write, take care of and entertain others straight away by using the skills and strengths you already have. You might be able to teach someone at work how to do something on the computer, or you might write a few lines of a poem or story every few days. That way you're still teaching or writing purposefully. When your sense of purpose is ingrained into your daily actions rather than some big dream, you can more readily find harmony between what you hope to achieve and what you are already doing.

Doing what you can with what you have is enough. Trying your best is enough. And the more you can balance productivity with pausing, and balance planning with acceptance that curve balls may screw up schedules, the more you'll feel that you are doing enough.

CHAPTER NINE

Looking Enough

Hands up if you have a stunningly beautiful friend who thinks they look terrible? I'm always amazed when I take a selection of group photographs and hear, "Ooh, not that one – I look horrendous!" Or, "No way, what's my mouth doing? Please don't share that one!" But when I look at the same photo, everybody looks amazing! It seems that, in general, we all think we look worse than we actually do.

Do you find yourself cringing at photographs of yourself or judging yourself negatively when you look in the mirror – noticing your flaws rather than your fabulousness? If you do, you're certainly not alone. In fact, it's rare to find someone who is completely happy with every inch of their body and how they look. Even those we'd think surely would be often aren't, because even the most beautiful people aren't immune from insecurity.

Negative body image is perhaps one of the most vocal critics of whether we are good enough. That feeling of not looking good enough can be like a constant pollutant, which gets in the way of life satisfaction.

It's a common habit to criticize our looks, rudely shame our bodies and relentlessly pick on our body parts, hating on ourselves. But this can lead from a sense of mild dissatisfaction of not looking good enough to incredibly destructive diseases like anorexia, bulimia and depression. Yet we are (once again) evaluating our looks based on inaccurate perceptions.

Mirror, Mirror

When you look at yourself in the mirror or in a photograph, you are peering at yourself stood there staring back at you (or the camera). You are static. This is not something that other people tend to see. You don't stand around in a static pose often. The version of you that other people get to see is the vibrant you, the you who is moving through your life, smiling and laughing, raising an eyebrow, looking puzzled, warmly nodding with encouragement, clapping your hands together, looking surprised, running your fingers through your hair, sparkling, giggling, animated, saying something funny or interesting or silly. They get to see the motion picture version of you and to witness more of your essence than you see when you look in the mirror or at a photo. So those harsh criticisms of what we look like aren't wholly accurate. What's more, they are also based, once again, on those external, rigid and limited pesky societal "shoulds".

Impossible ideals

We are bombarded with images of idealized beauty – and these images are incredibly limited and dependent on what's fashionable at the time. In the 1990s there was "heroin chic", which promoted pale and uber-skinny as beautiful, while these days we're revisiting the 1950s ideal with women expected to have big boobs and bums and small waists and legs (an almost impossible paradox). Meanwhile the pressure on men is to look like lean bodybuilders with #EverydayAbs. But hardly any of us actually look like coiffed and buffed *Love Island* contestants.

These expectations of female flawlessness and male machoism are causing men and women alike to experience deep body insecurities. When I was growing up, those images came from the airbrushed covers of magazines, television or billboard adverts and music videos. Nowadays they shine out constantly from the screens of the devices we keep in our pockets and take everywhere with us. These images of perfection – filtered and edited so much that they're not even real – follow us around wherever we go, a relentless restrictive and unrealistic ideal of what beauty *should* look like.

By internalizing these particularly limited shackles of should, we start to believe that you can only be beautiful if you measure up, quite literally, to those expectations: we should be young, we should have a certain bushiness of eyebrow or sleekness of hair. These beauty standards are, essentially, bullshit. How do I know this? Because the majority of us will never look like this – thank goodness!

Sameness vs uniqueness

We're not meant to look the same. Everybody's body is different – frizzy and fuzzy or spotty and cuddly or gangly and pointy – and that's where our beauty really lies, in our difference.

We each have different shaped faces and ears and noses and lips and that's a good thing. It would be such a boring yawnfest (and very weird) if we all looked identical. Yet we buy into this rigid standard of beauty and we buy all these "solutions" to help us solve problems that don't exist. We don't need to change our faces to look the same as other people – our own beauty is in our individuality. That's the only beauty standard to hold ourselves up to – our difference *is* our beauty.

All bodies are good bodies. No matter what they look like. And it's so important to have mutual respect for all shapes, sizes, colours and types, to celebrate diversity. We need diversity of thought, of people, of ethnicity, of capability, of looks and strengths, in order for humanity to thrive.

Thankfully, over the past few years, different ideals of beauty have been held up as viable – curvy, shapely and #FiercelyReal images have made their way into mainstream media and more plus-size models are being used in fashion campaigns, so the shackles are loosening and the options improving to include more realistic and relatable versions of what constitutes beautiful.

Still, in order to feel like you look good enough, it's important to ignore what Instagram says you *should* look like, or what those airbrushed front pages of glossy magazines offer up as the perfect version of beauty. Or even what your inner critic pipes up when comparing the static, badly lit version of you it sees when you look in the mirror to well put-together friends with shiny hair and nice teeth.

The human body is incredible

Your body is amazing! That is a fact about your body rather than an inaccurate perception or assumption, so let's take a moment to marvel at your awesomeness. Your body is made up of 37 trillion cells and 78 organs, the main five (heart, brain, kidneys, liver and lungs) all working to keep you alive each day.

The pupils in our eyes shrink or grow to let in more light. Our blood is filtered by our body more than 300 times every single day. Our bones, ounce for ounce, are stronger than steel. If we break a bone or fall and bang our knees, our bodies spring into action and begin the healing process, inflaming to protect the injured area that needs to heal. Some parts of our bodies harbour good bacteria which fight infection and, when we're poorly, our body automatically raises our temperature to help fight off those infections. Even having a moderate amount of fat reserves can be useful as we get older or ill, because those reserves store energy.

Our bodies and minds are built to take care of us, and given how hard they work to do so, isn't it time we repaid the favour and took care of and appreciated them? What if we decided, right here, to show our bodies some respect rather than dissing them so much? What if, rather than wait until your body stops working to start appreciating how amazing it is, you started to take pleasure and feel gratitude for how your body works and feels and how you look right now? To be thankful that you get to move parts of your body, that you can, that you are able, and to love every unique part of you.

Come on, let's rebel!

Of course, it doesn't serve the beauty and wellness industries for you to be content with the way your face looks, or to be happy with your body, or to be mentally and physically flourishing, to optimally function, the way you were designed to be. So what if we all challenged these industries with a rebellious act of self-appreciation and self-respect? I say, be a rebel. Like yourself!

Unfortunately, there's a dark side to these industries as they can prey on our insecurities about what we look like, with the promise of looking younger and prettier and getting slimmer and buffer. So we buy lip-fillers and bum-lifters and waist-trainers which, when they don't magically transform us into Insta-ready goddesses, make us feel even worse than we did before we shelled out our hard-earned cash on them.

Those industries have a lot to lose if we all started to like ourselves the way we are and saw how we looked as good enough, thank you very much. Indeed, the amount spent on beauty products and weight-loss programmes is a testament to how much we collectively want to change our bodies and improve how we look. But for whom?

By 2023, the diet industry is expected to be worth over $270 billion, while the global cosmetics industry (worth over $500 billion in 2018) is predicted to be worth more than $758.4 billion by 2025. We're collectively investing a lot of pounds into losing pounds and changing our appearance.

Of course, sometimes we wear make-up to enhance and celebrate our looks, just as going to the gym can be as much about keeping fit and feeling good as it is about slimming down or firming up. Those are healthy reasons for investing in ourselves – to empower ourselves, celebrate who we are and take care of our bodies. And that's the key here – how we feel about our bodies and our looks comes down to our attitude about them.

There's this judgement spectrum which, at its most harmful end is mostly critical and judgemental, harming our self-esteem. At the other end is curiosity and acceptance – feeling like we look good enough – and that's the end of the spectrum to try to reach.

STEP 30: GET CURIOUS

I have a tattoo on the inside of each wrist. One is a pause button to remind me to pause often and to pause before responding – the latter is a work in progress! The second tattoo features the text, "I wonder..." – I had this permanently inked on my skin to remind me to stay curious and consider what a different way of looking at something might be.

Curiosity allows us to think with greater flexibility and let go of what no longer serves us mentally. Curiosity opens the door to compassion. Take our desire to change the way we look. This can either come from a place of lack, of "not good enough", or from a place of care, of wanting to change for the right reasons. So get curious about why looking good enough matters to you. When you swap judgement for curiosity about why you're judging yourself so harshly, you give yourself space to consider alternative ways of viewing and valuing yourself.

+ Let go of unattainable ideals and get curious about the possibilities and positive what-ifs. When you do this, you give yourself the freedom to be more flexible and content with whatever reality emerges. For example, one of mine: "I should get rid of these moles on my chin" can be replaced with "I wonder... should I really? Who says? They're a part of me, so I say they stay for now." Or, talking of chins: "I hate my double chin" becomes "I wonder... would I feel this way if everyone else had a double chin too? I doubt it. Having multiple chinnage does not make me a bad person and I'm not going to let that one thing make me feel bad." In fact, I could go as far as reminding myself: "Today I've met a deadline, cooked a scrummy meal and made someone I love feel better – frankly *that* matters more than my chin(s)."

✦ Let go of the notion that having the ideal body or appearance will somehow solve all your problems and make you happier. How you look is not related to your value or your health. People who fit the ideal of beauty are not immune from hardships or sadness. Everyone, even people who appear to have it all, is fighting their own battles. Indeed, the size of someone's body or the attractiveness of someone's face doesn't indicate how healthy or unhealthy, how happy or unhappy they are. You can be slender and ill, and you can be on the larger side physically yet be healthy, fit and strong. What's more, physical health is just one part of our overall health. Mental health is equally as important and that's invisible. You generally can't tell how mentally well someone is from their appearance – smiles can hide pain.

If you have a desire to improve how you look, get curious about where that desire comes from. What's motivating that need? Is it because you want more people to like you and think looking good will result in that outcome? Is it because you think you'll have a better chance of attracting a partner? Or is it because you want more energy and want to feel healthier and more alert?

If it's the first or second reason, get curious about the facts. Do you like stunningly beautiful people more than you like the rest of us? Do you prefer hanging out with people who fit societal ideals of beauty? Chances are the answer to those questions is "no", because you're not shallow. You like people because of how they treat you, how they make you feel and whether they make you laugh. And while partners are attracted to each other initially because of appearance, it's everything else that keeps people together, beyond looks alone. If, however, your desire to change is about wanting more energy and vitality, then it's not about looking good after all – it's about feeling good, and that is a healthy motivating factor.

STEP 31: SHIFT YOUR MINDSET TO FOCUS ON FEELING AND FUNCTIONALITY

Simple shifts of attitude can make a big difference to how you feel about your body and what you do with it. Instead of focusing on what your body looks like (too much this or not enough that), shift your focus toward how your body feels (strong, tired and so on) and what it actually does (its purpose and functionality). For example, your arms are for lifting and hugging, your legs for getting you from A to B. The size of them is important for what they enable you to do, rather than what they look like.

✦ Focus on vitality. Do things which increase your energy and strength levels and make you feel good. This is a great way to develop body acceptance and move toward body celebration as you begin to feel grateful for feeling energized. Physical strength can give you a sense of inner badassery that makes you feel like titanium – in a throw-whatever-you-have-at-me kind of way. This can be powerful when it comes to countering negative thoughts about how you look, because you *feel* strong.

✦ Connect with your body. Try this exercise: Slowly lift your hands up in front of your face. Turn them over and regard your palms. Say, "These are my hands." Next stretch up tall and imagine space flowing in between each vertebrae of your spine. Then put your hands on your hips. Say, "This is my body." Finally give your cheeks a gentle squeeze and your body a gentle hug. Say "Thank you, body." The deeper the connection we have for our bodies, the more compelled we feel to take good care of them. The more you are able to tune in to your body, the better you get at trusting what it is telling you. By connecting with your body, you open a conversation with it about what you need and how you want to move.

✦ Think about how you do and don't want to feel and write those words down. For example, "I want to feel... energetic, alive, free, happy, alert, strong. I don't want to feel... tired, frustrated, disappointed, guilty." Think about what kind of movement might help you feel less of what you don't want and more of what you do. Dancing, taking a nature walk, climbing a tree, ice skating, playing tag with your kids or friends? Schedule these types of movement into your day because of the way it will make you feel, rather than because of the way it might make you look.

✦ Move your body in a way that you enjoy. Your body (and mind) will thank you for it. Do the kind of exercise you want to do that makes you feel good, not what you "should" be doing because it's good for you. We don't have to cart our wobbly bums* off to the gym if we absolutely hate gyms. There are so many different ways to move our bodies that are brilliant for them – from wild swimming and paddle boarding to roller skating and pole dancing. *(I speak for myself in reference to bums. My daughter once "lovingly" referred to my bottom as looking like two planets, while simultaneously pleading with me not to lose weight because I wouldn't be cuddly anymore – not cuddly enough – I see the irony there.)

I once had a moment of clarity and connection during a yoga session where I felt especially in tune with my body and felt like apologizing to it for not taking good care of it recently. I say recently, I actually mean since leaving school 30 years ago. This moment of connection and realization about what I owed to my body, which has been taking care of me for 47 years, provided the catalyst for me to change my habits and start looking after my body better. These gentle shifts in attitude have the power to set you free, so you can use the time you used to waste wishing you looked different and fixating on food and instead focus on more helpful thoughts and ideas.

STEP 32: DEVELOP AN ATTITUDE OF BODY ACCEPTANCE AND CELEBRATION

Celebrate your body. Celebrate the bits of you which make you unlike any other person. Celebrate those parts of you that you've inherited, and which therefore make you part of a family. Shift how you view those features.

✦ Make peace with your body rather than be at war with it. Each time you say you hate a certain part of your body or think you don't look good enough, that's what you're doing – fighting against your own body, you're fighting against yourself. Resolve not to fight with yourself anymore. If it helps, write it down: "I'm sorry, body, I promise to stop hating you because... you're the only one I've got... you help me do what I need to do in my daily life... you're keeping me alive... you're great at protecting me... you're amazing!"

✦ Focus on developing respect and admiration for the way you look. If you don't love your body, that's okay. If you struggle to accept your body, that's okay, as long as you do respect your body and care for it. Respecting and caring for your body is enough. You don't need to think you're stunningly gorgeous. You don't even need to think you're particularly attractive. You only need to show your body the respect it deserves. That's a great first step toward feeling good enough.

✦ Shift how you view ageing. This is something I feel especially passionate about. We grumble so much about getting older, yet growing old is a privilege denied to so many. I can say this with a depth of feeling because both my parents died young. My mum was 43 when she passed away and my dad was 67. You may know someone who passed away at a young age, someone who would give anything to have more time to live and grow old, who would cherish the chance to get wrinkles and grey hair. Consider that the next time you complain about ageing or buy something to try to mask the process that so many did not get the opportunity to live through.

We are the lucky ones. We get to LIVE thanks to our incredibly powerful and wonderful bodies. When we start to see our bodies as good enough, we can get on with rewarding them for all their hard work – by enjoying life, being happy in our own stretchy, resilient and remarkable skin.

CHAPTER TEN

Feeling Enough

Looking good enough, doing well enough, having and being enough – all these measures of how we perceive we are doing at life – come back to one other ultimate benchmark, how good we *feel* and whether we feel satisfied enough with how our lives are going. Our level of life satisfaction tells us whether we feel good enough or not. When we feel lacking in the areas mentioned in this book, the pendulum of general enoughness can swing toward dissatisfaction. That feeling on its own can be tough to cope with. But add to that the pressure to be happy and, if you're not feeling in a relatively consistent state of joy, you can feel like you're not doing very well at life, which only adds to the pressure of trying to live up to impossible standards. Yet constant happiness is a myth. Sustainable well-being isn't about being constantly joyful or denying negative feelings, rather, true contentment is about cherishing the good and coping with the bad.

Move the happiness goal posts

As human beings with the capacity to feel a whole spectrum of emotions, feeling mostly happy is an unrealistic expectation. Even the most positive people cannot sustain happiness every single day.

Take yours truly. As a positive psychology practitioner and author, I write books about well-being, happiness and resilience and I run workshops to help people fret less and flourish more. I do this work because, having experienced loss, I want to help people make the most of their precious lives and know that they are good enough. For the past seven years I've studied what helps people stay "north of neutral" and for the most part, I practise what I preach – I go on regular gratitude walks and get out in nature, I make time for some non-negotiable self-care rituals, and I spend time doing what I love with people I love to help me sustain a decent level of well-being. People who know me well tell me I'm a positive person and my VIA signature strengths (see page 52) are hope and optimism, gratitude and zest.

Yet, of course, from time to time, I crash. I hold my hand vulnerably up to say I sometimes cry in the shower when things feel overwhelming or when I'm missing my parents. I've suffered major hardships – losing my amazing mother when I was 17 being the main one, and I experience disappointments and arguments and all the other stuff that can bring us down. I feel frustrated, annoyed and misunderstood sometimes too. Why? Because I'm human. Feeling these feelings does not erase all the good in my life. Feeling *meh* from time to time is the norm. Because life really is a rollercoaster with many ups and downs, so feeling *occasionally* happy and grateful *sometimes* is enough.

With this is mind, in order to feel good enough, it's important we modify our expectations around happiness. Because you can't feel good all the time. Feeling enough means accepting that truth, rather than expecting the impossible.

Focusing on positivity and forbidding negativity can be as counter-productive to our actual happiness as focusing on perfection and ignoring reality. That's the paradox of positivity. We need to be realistic. Boosting our well-being isn't about increasing pleasure and removing pain, that's not how our brains work. It's about developing a realistic sense of optimism, finding balance between our emotions and letting go of notions of "the perfect life". And while it's important for us to counter our negativity bias – i.e., to tackle those inflexible and inaccurate negative *thoughts* which can unreasonably pull us down, there is room for genuinely real and accurate negative *feelings*. Because feelings are true; thoughts aren't always. And that's the difference – negativity bias is about negative thoughts and beliefs, often untrue ones that unfairly adversely affect how we show up in the world. Negative *feelings*, on the other hand, are true and real and belong to us and are therefore worth listening to.

Whenever you think or you believe or you know; you're a lot of other people: but the moment you feel, you're nobody-but-yourself.

E. E. Cummings

STEP 33: SEE THE POWER IN ADVERSITY AND EMOTIONAL SIGNALS

Living a good life doesn't come from sailing through life with no problems, it comes from weathering the storm and rising from the depths, solving problems and overcoming obstacles. That's engaging in real life, and that's where our strength and sense of accomplishment often come from.

A happy life consists not in the absence, but in the mastery of hardships.

Helen Keller

This is why, in our quest for happiness, we must give unhappiness a seat at the table, because unhappiness and struggle are an important part of what it means to be human and both positive and negative emotions can strengthen us.

Here's the science bit: positive emotions are useful because they literally grow our capacity for coping. As Barbara Fredrickson discovered in her research on positivity, positive emotions essentially act as building blocks, which broaden our minds to enable more effective behaviour when responding to trauma and stress.[11] This means that the more positive emotions we feel over time, the more "positivity reserves" we have in our well-being bank account, which we can draw upon during difficult times to help us bounce back better, bolstering our resilience.

Positivity literally opens our minds and helps us think more clearly. Conversely, negative emotions can close down our cognitive functioning, so we can find ourselves less open to figuring out potential solutions. That said, negative emotions can also be useful.

Adversity strengthens

Indeed, experiencing hardships and the subsequent negative emotions they bring can strengthen us and give us more confidence in our ability to cope. Professor Martin Seligman and Dr Chris Peterson, founding fathers of positive psychology, conducted a survey of 1,700 people alongside a well-being measurement test.[12] They listed 15 of the worst possible adversities that can happen to a person in a lifetime and asked respondents to tick those they had experienced. They discovered those who had experienced one of the adversities showed more acute mental strength and greater well-being than those who had not.

Even more surprisingly, those who had experienced three adversities were mentally stronger than those who had endured two, who in turn were stronger than those who had been through one. This study, along with research about post-traumatic growth, reveals that enduring setbacks can be incredibly empowering as our self-belief and resilience often rises the more we've demonstrated what we can cope with.

In this way, the hardships we go through often teach us, always shape us and frequently improve us. And we certainly learn more from the hardships we experience than from the rosy moments of life. This realization that all experiences and feelings count can help us see that all feelings are enough, as even tough ones offer growth and resilience.

No rainbows without rain

We are the sum of all we have endured and experienced. Adversity, mistakes, regrets and tragedy – difficult as they are – can all teach us something useful and we need them in our lives. They not only show us what we are capable of coping with but also provide sufficient contrast, so that we can appreciate the good times. In this way negative emotions can be as useful as they are brutal.

Like flowers, we need rain as much as sunshine in order to flourish. If we expect only sunshine, we're less equipped to cope when the rain pours down on us – as it will, and often does. Such contrast enables us to better view our lives through a lens of gratitude. For when things aren't going well, we're better able to notice and appreciate when things are.

✦ Think about a hardship you've been through – something really tough. Now think about what that has taught you about yourself. How has enduring that hardship and emerging the other side shaped you? Consider how it might have improved you, as it likely has. The realization that, even when worst-case scenarios do happen, we can somehow cope, learn and appreciate more, can reduce the weight of worries as we remind ourselves that we can and will handle what life throws at us.

✦ Don't feel bad about feeling bad. Next time you're feeling down, give yourself permission to be human and allow it. Remind yourself there is power in feeling down as it is helping you release what needs to be released. What's more, your feelings could be guiding you toward making some changes in your life that will make you feel better. For example, if you're feeling lonely, that would signal the need to do something to deepen existing relationships or develop some new ones.

✦ Follow the signposts. Tune in to your feelings to help you figure out when to stop, continue in the same direction or change route. In this way your feelings are like your own personal GPS system. Negative emotions can act as useful signals and catalysts for change, while positive emotions are signalling for you to do more of whatever you're doing. Ask yourself what your sadness, fear or anger might be signalling to you about what to do next.

✦ Keep it real. Free yourself from the social pressure about not feeling sad and show your vulnerable side from time to time. Sharing our gritty truth can actually make other people relate to us on a deeper level and connect us with other people experiencing similar difficulties, as long as it's balanced with sharing joys. Knowing we are not alone in feeling a certain way can make us feel better and supported.

✦ Pop the beach ball. Striving for a perfect life where we push negative emotions to one side is like trying to push a beach ball below the water and expecting it to stay down. It won't – it will resurface. You need to pop the beach ball and the only way to do that is to feel the feelings or reframe negative thoughts (see page 73). So lean in to what you are feeling. Allow yourself time to cry or feel angry or sad. Label your feelings (see page 49) and then express them by letting them out. Suppression and repression of emotions can do more harm than good, whereas expression of emotions allows us to move through them, onward and upward.

STEP 34: TACKLE ANXIETY AND RUMINATION TO ENJOY NOW

Spending a lot of time worrying about the future and/or ruminating about the past can stop us from enjoying the now, which can cause us to feel like we are not living a good enough life. But there are ways to reduce anxiety and rumination.

Worries can lead to catastrophic thinking and downward spirals, but they simply start off as thoughts about something that has yet to happen. So, to reduce anxiety:

✦ Gain perspective. Consider whatever you're worrying about, and run through the worst-case, best-case and most likely scenarios. For example, perhaps you've missed a mortgage payment and worry about what might happen.

✦ First imagine the worst-case scenario. For example, that you miss more payments and end up having your house repossessed and end up homeless. Now give the likelihood of that happening a percentage (e.g., one per cent).

✦ Next imagine the wildly best-case scenario. It could be that you win a significant sum of money which enables you to pay off your entire mortgage, not just next month's payment. Again, give the likelihood of that happening a percentage. (e.g., one per cent).

✦ Now consider the most-likely-case scenario. That, after talking to your lender, you figure out a way to commit to reduced payments for a few months to help you get back on track. The likelihood of this would be more like 98 per cent. So you can now rein in those negative spirals of doom and breathe a sigh of relief.

✦ Breathe. Whenever you feel anxious, in order to protect you from the imagined harm, your brain fires up the emotional part of your brain (the amygdala) and gets you into fight-or-flight mode. This means you literally cannot access the rational part of your brain where logical thought takes place (the pre-frontal cortex) because that part has been shut down in order to give all your resources to the fight-or-flight part. It's like a security guard stopping you from entering the building to sort out the (frequently non-existent) situation. So you can end up getting in a right state imagining the worst and unable to logically problem-solve. The only way to access the logical part of the brain is to calm down. There are different ways to return to this calm state. You can try breathing slowly in and out, inhaling for four and exhaling for six – the longer outer breath helps get you back to a more relaxed state. Another method is to give your cognitive thinking brain something to focus on, such as counting. You could try counting backward from 100 in sevens or count the number of red cars that drive past. These techniques can help you gain control and bring yourself back to rational thinking mode.

Ruminating on things that have been said or done can lead to strong feelings of guilt and sadness. But there are ways to pull ourselves out of this judgemental thought process:

✦ Learn, adapt and move on. Ruminating on the past can lead us down a rabbit hole of blame and shame, yet the past has happened and we cannot change it. All we can do is learn from our mistakes and regrets to help us make better choices in the future. See the value in learning such valuable lessons on your life's journey. Then move on.

✦ Focus on the present moment. Whenever you notice yourself ruminating on past regrets or worrying about the future, bring yourself back to now. Ground yourself in the moment – revisit page 94 to make the most of where you are presently and savour that.

Knowing that adversities and hardships can be useful to diffuse our fear and anxiety, while grasping that our poorest decisions and worst responses offer useful knowledge, can help us accept our mistakes. Realizing that our challenges often lead to growth can help us feel more at ease with riding with the more difficult emotions, and letting them guide us in the direction we hope to go in.

PART THREE

SELF

Your relationship with yourself sets the tone for every other relationship you have.

Robert Holden

You can't hate your way into liking yourself. Telling yourself what a failure you are won't make you any more successful. Telling yourself you're not living up to your full potential won't help you reach a higher potential. Telling yourself you're worthless and unlovable won't make you feel any more worthy or lovable. I know it sounds almost annoyingly simple, but the only way to achieve self-love is to love yourself – regardless of who you are and where you stand and even if you know you want to change.

You are enough just as you are. And self-love will be a little bit easier every time you remind yourself of that. In order to truly like and/or love yourself, you need to accept who you are, believe in yourself and have compassion for yourself when you get things wrong and when things don't work out as you'd hoped. This is the ABC of enoughness and what the remaining few chapters of this book will focus on.

CHAPTER ELEVEN

Self-Acceptance

The most important and enduring relationship you have is the one you have with yourself, because that is who you are going to spend the rest of your life with. Your level of self-acceptance and approval will depend on your own life experiences, how deeply you've internalized them and how you choose to respond to them (although the latter can be a work in progress). For example, if you've had an absent parent or one who constantly criticized you and demanded perfection or showed favouritism or neglected you, or if you've experienced trauma or abuse or rejection over your lifetime, you may have internalized the inaccurate belief that you are not enough. Similarly, if you've had a teacher or a sibling or other influential person constantly criticize you, thinking you are not enough may have become a firm belief.

Young humans who don't get the love or approval they are meant to get (and deserve to have) simply by virtue of being born, can have difficulty realizing that the problem was not with them, but with the person who made them feel like they weren't lovable enough. When you're young you don't have the life experience to realize that a parent's or peer's lack of approval stems from *their* issues, rather than yours. Back then, when those feelings of not-enoughness were internalized you didn't know enough about life to know that it wasn't your fault that you were treated this way, so you may have ended up blaming yourself and feeling shame as a result.

Deeply held beliefs that stem from childhood like this then become reinforced by society and the media, by unattainable beauty standards, relationship ideals and academic expectations, which perpetuate this belief of not being enough. This is why even those who did receive love from parents and support from teachers may still have internalized beliefs that they are not enough from the wide array of self-squishing sources that surround us.

Gardening

The only way to tackle the feeling of not being enough is to un-root that deeply rooted belief. You need to pull out the weeds (the *false* belief that you are not enough) and plant the seed (the *factual* belief that you are enough) so you may accept who you are and flourish. To do that you need to know where the weeds are planted so you can dig up the root, to go back in time to find the root cause – the point in time when you internalized the belief that you weren't enough. If you can't remember a specific event or time period, that's okay. It may have been a general way of being spoken to or being treated in a certain way consistently.

You then need to take those thoughts of not-enoughness to court – just like you did during the Inner Critic Challenge – to explore where they came from and realize they aren't facts. The only reason you may believe them to be true is because you've repeated those thoughts often enough to become beliefs, which become mental schemas and affect how we behave and show up in the world. This can then confirm judgemental thoughts about ourselves and so it continues.

Whose belief is it anyway?

If you do have shame that stems from your childhood, that, like other beliefs you may have internalized, is NOT YOUR SHAME. It belongs to someone else and you have merely learned it. As a learned belief it has created a learned behaviour, which means it can be unlearned. Hurrah for that!

Unfortunately, many people go through life trying to fill the gaps and numb the pain that being bereft of love and approval has created. In order to gain approval, they strive for success and aim for wealth, to prove to those people and themselves that they are enough. However, as psychologists and therapists have discovered, no amount of success or fame can counter these deep-rooted feelings, which explains why many super successful stars end up with destructive or self-sabotaging behaviours, like addiction. Because, when you achieve and accumulate a lot of success but *still* feel that sense of not being enough, the pain intensifies, so all you can do is try to numb the pain.

Thankfully, that is not all you can do if you have lived your life feeling like you are not enough – even though, by virtue of existing, you *are*. Remember, you have simply learned beliefs based on other people's bad behaviour and blamed yourself as deficient, rather than seeing the other person as the one with the unresolved issues. They behaved in that way because of beliefs they had about themselves as being not deserving or unlovable and other beliefs they learned from their parents and influencers, and so on and so forth. So we end up with these deep-rooted beliefs that don't belong to us but have been learned and ingrained. Doing this first step – digging up the roots of beliefs, questioning them and realizing that they weren't yours in the first place and are not based on fact – is crucial.

Supplanting the old with the new

Next, write a list of any other limiting beliefs you may have that relate to you not being enough or that cause you shame. For example, by way of sharing my own vulnerabilities, mine might be: I'm not fit enough, I'm not patient enough, I'm not tidy enough, I'm not a good enough parent, I'm not a good enough friend and so on.

Now rewrite your list in a way that questions and supplants those thoughts. For example: It's not necessarily that I'm not good enough as a parent, but it's true to say I don't always lay down the law as strictly as I probably ought to. But that doesn't mean I'm not a good enough parent because, actually, my daughter is very much loved, encouraged, and honest and we spend a lot of time talking and laughing and I try to balance focusing on her strengths with inevitable nagging and we have a close relationship. So, in fact, I am a good parent.

Now it's your turn to do the same on a piece of paper, to write down your own "not-enough" thoughts, what makes you think you aren't enough and what is true and not necessarily true about those thoughts? Remember to expand on this by inserting a positive fact which counters your initial claim of shame and finish with a positive opposite to your initial "not enough" statement. Once you've weeded out those detrimental weeds, you can start to plant a garden that will enable you to flourish.

You have been criticizing yourself for years, and it hasn't worked. Try approving of yourself and see what happens.

Louise L. Hay

Planting the seeds of self-acceptance

Seeds of self-acceptance bloom into feelings of self-approval as you grow to like yourself and can more readily flourish. When you don't like yourself it's easy to create a life you don't particularly like either, which acts as a self-fulfilling prophecy that you aren't enough and don't deserve to live a good life.

In contrast, when you *do* like yourself – when you accept and appreciate who you are and know that you *are* enough – life can be wonderful (even when days are difficult). Because how much you accept and approve of yourself will shift how you view your life, especially how you view your life when things inevitably don't go to plan.

For example, daily tasks that were "torturous" will become annoying but achievable and those pesky administrative chores will go from being "absolute hell" to "an opportunity to get the more arduous tasks out of the way". And this is important because the way you feel about yourself comes down to the words you say to yourself and the stories you tell yourself. Those words have the power to shape your reality.

Now, we've already dug up the weeds with the deepest roots (those beliefs internalized during childhood) and supplanted a few more weeds with positive seedlings. Now it's time to plant a new seed for a wonderful giant sunflower that will stand in the middle of your mind's garden. To counter the weed of "I am not enough", you need to plant a seed which says, "I AM ENOUGH." And you then need to water it (repeat it) often. To do that:

✦ Write "I am enough" on sticky notes and pop them wherever you will see them often – in the corner of your laptop screen, on your mirror, on your fridge. Have fun with it and paint or sew the words "I am enough" and display them as pieces of art. Start each day by writing "I am enough" a few times on a notepad. Doodle it or just write it. Literally give yourself lines but make it fun. After a while, your brain will start to believe what you are saying and thinking and writing, because you've repeated that thought often. Remember, beliefs are simply thoughts that have been repeated often, so the more you repeat that factual statement, you carve out a new neural pathway which becomes a belief (just like your old thoughts became beliefs through you repeating them so often). "I am enough" is a statement of fact, because you are enough simply because you exist.

✦ Share #IAmEnough and #YouAreEnough hashtags on social media to claim your enoughness and our enoughness and share it with the world. Hashtag #YouAreEnoughBook for me and readers of this book to comment with encouraging words.

✦ Say out loud: "This shame/belief doesn't belong to me. It's not my shame/belief. It came from someone else. I can let it go now. I am enough. Nobody else has the power to make me feel less than my inherent value. I am enough simply because I exist." Repeat this a few times now and whenever you feel that sense of not-enoughness or shame popping up.

Do you take sugar?

The good news is, although it can take some effort to create new mental habits and learn to like who you are, that's still far less effort than it takes to try to be somebody you're not. Good mental habits are a bit like stopping having sugar in your tea – it's weird at first but, before long, tea with sugar tastes too sweet because you've habitually got used to having tea without. Over time you've altered your taste and got used to the new way. Similarly, the more you repeat thoughts they become beliefs that you are enough, and the more you habitually get used to pausing to question inaccurate beliefs, the easier it becomes.

CHAPTER TWELVE

Self-Belief

Bravery to see possibilities and seize opportunities takes self-belief. It takes self-efficacy to say, "I am capable enough to do this", to rise to this challenge, to step outside my comfort zone, to put in the effort and to go against the grain. Self-belief is critical to feeling good enough.

The key two words when it comes to self-belief are "I am." And the opposite of self-belief is self-doubt. Of course, everyone has moments of self-doubt from time to time. As we've already learned, between 70–80 per cent of people experience imposter syndrome at some point in their lives. So we need to remind ourselves of our positive "I ams" and reconsider our negative ones.

When your view of yourself is driven by self-doubt and shame, you'll think: "I am no good," rather than, "I didn't do well this time." Or you'll think, "I am a failure," rather than "I failed this time, but I can learn from it." The former way of thinking is pessimistic – that's an explanatory style which attributes success to being a fluke or coincidence and not attributable to you, and failures as being your own fault due to your incapability. Pessimistic thinking means failures are seen as long-lasting and all-encompassing whereas successes are seen as unlikely to last and specific.

Conversely, if you're an optimistic thinker you'll tend to see the successes you have as being down to your own efforts which can be sustained and can positively impact other areas of life. Whereas you'll see failures as temporary and specific and, if as a result of your own lack of effort, you'll accept that and try harder next time.

Negative judgements can create doubts and insecurities, which disable us and can prevent us from trying new potentially enjoyable experiences or from bouncing back from adversity. You think, "I'll never get that promotion because I'm not good enough so there's no point even applying for it." Whereas, optimistic thinking will lead you to go for the promotion and, if you're unsuccessful, to try harder next time. Believing you can is the difference.

Reframing limiting beliefs with empowering ones

✦ Create a list of positive "I ams". Consider times when you thought you couldn't do something but you did it. Then write it down. For example, "I held a tarantula in my hand at the local zoo and faced my fear of spiders, which means I am brave." (True story.) Or "I wrote that blog on a topic I thought I couldn't write, which means I am a resourceful writer." Or "I delivered a well-received workshop I was nervous about delivering, which means I am capable of speaking in public."

✦ Replace "I can't" (a weed) with "I can" (a seed) and flourish. So replace, "I can't cope, I can't do it" with "I can cope and I can do it." Make reframed comments realistic and neutral so they are believable but still positive. For example, replace, "I can't cope with this, I'm terrible at it and I'm never going to be good at it," with "I can cope with this, I've been struggling and finding it hard but, with practice I can improve."

✦ Fake it 'til you make it. It is possible to trick your brain into feeling differently, especially when two different feelings have similar "symptoms" in the body. Take nervousness and excitement, for example. When you physically feel nervous, you get the same sweaty palms, quickened heartbeat and feeling of butterflies in your stomach as you do when you're excited. So, when you're feeling nervous and not good enough and think you can't do something, tell your mind, "I'm really excited," and picture other times when you've felt similarly excited, and you'll begin to switch that negative nervous feeling with a more positive feeling of anticipation. The same is true when you tell yourself, "I can do this," and strike a power pose with your hands on your hips and your head held high, even when you're scared. Your brain will believe that you can and so you will.

✦ Go on adventures. Taking calculated risks and doing something you didn't think you could do is a confidence booster and proves to your inner critic that you are capable. Activities like rock-climbing, kayaking and exploring often show you that you can do a great deal more than you thought you could. So going on adventures will help you to generate greater self-belief by default. Replace self-doubt with idea-doubt. According to Adam Grant, author of *Originals: How Non-Conformists Move the World*, there are two kinds of doubt: self-doubt, which can stop us from doing things and make us give up, or idea doubt, which can motivate us to accept that first drafts of ideas aren't likely to be the best versions and to keep going.[13] Next time you feel some doubt creeping in, shift it toward the latter type and try again.

✦ Reassess. Ask yourself, "Am I trying my best?" and "Am I learning from my mistakes?" If you can say, "I am trying my best" and "I am learning from my mistakes", then you are doing enough, and your self-doubt can be replaced with self-belief.

CHAPTER THIRTEEN

Self-Compassion

Rather than wondering and worrying whether we are good enough, how about we shift our focus to being good enough to ourselves? That's what self-compassion is all about.

Self-compassion is different to self-esteem. When we have good self-esteem, it means we feel good about ourselves when we're doing well. When we have good self-compassion, we feel good about ourselves even when (especially when) we're *not* doing so well. Self-esteem tends to desert us when we need it the most, when we've failed spectacularly at something. In contrast, self-compassion allows us to fail without judgement, because self-compassion is about giving ourselves permission to be human.

Self-compassion knows that being perfect is not being human. Being flawed is. It knows we don't need to have everything figured out and that getting things wrong doesn't automatically make you not good enough, it just makes you a normal human-being. Self-compassion is great at giving you a break. Self-compassion listens and notices your needs so it can figure out how best to give you the support and care it knows you deserve. And, as a consequence of showing ourselves compassion we needn't rely on others to feel good about ourselves. Bonus!

Set the scene for compassion

Before we can make self-compassion a habitual response, we need to get used to the idea of having more empathy for our own experiences in the way we do for others. To do so, it's worth spending some time in creating a kind of compassionate energy field – getting ourselves into a compassionate frame of mind.

Practise a "loving kindness" meditation. The ancient meditation of compassion and loving kindness only takes a minute or two to run through but it's a wonderful way to send out compassionate energy before bringing that energy back to you. Take a minute every single morning (or evening), notice your pain, and silently wish for it to end. Wish for your own happiness. Then do the same for people you know.

✦ First, sit comfortably and breathe in slowly for a count of four and exhale slowly for a count of four. Repeat this a few times until you are feeling relaxed and, each time your mind wanders, bring it back to your breathing.

✦ Now bring to mind someone you care deeply for. This person could be someone in your life now or someone who has been in your life before. It could be a person or it could be a pet. As long as bringing this person to mind fills you with a sense of deep care and warmth. That feeling is loving kindness. Focus on that feeling for a moment and, in your mind's eye, see a warm ball of light surrounding your heart and emanating out to this person. As you picture that warm glow, say in your head or out loud: "May you be well, may you be safe from harm, may you live your life with ease, may you be happy," and watch that golden light flow from your heart to theirs.

✦ Next bring to mind someone you know who you don't have a particularly positive relationship with but who could still do with a dose of loving kindness. See that same golden light flowing from your heart to theirs as you repeat that same mantra.

✦ Repeat this mantra sending loving kindness out to your family and friends, and again to your local community and neighbours before repeating it again and directing that flow of loving kindness light to the wider world.

✦ Finally, direct this mantra to yourself as you place your hand on your heart. Say: "May you be well, may you be safe from harm, may you live your life with ease, may you be happy," meaning you. Inhale that feeling of compassion for yourself and visualize the warm glow of light radiating out from your heart to surround your body.

Be compassionate

Self-compassion is about comforting ourselves the way we comfort friends who are struggling. If your best friend was hurt and experiencing pain, you'd comfort them and they would deserve that comfort. Equally, you deserve to receive the same level of comfort from yourself. Yet we often fail to show ourselves the tender kindness, patience, and care that we give others. Let's change that.

✦ Have regular comfort check-ins with yourself. Whenever you are feeling low or start giving yourself a hard time, ask yourself, what do I need in this moment? Reassurance? Forgiveness? Acceptance? A nice cup of tea? A good long walk? Some stretchy yoga and a shower? Give yourself the comfort you need and deserve.

✦ Write a note that says, "I LOVE YOU". Put it on your mirror or laptop or wherever you do a morning HIIT workout or online yoga class. It's a love note to you from you and it's meant to make you smile.

✦ Remind yourself of your wonder. Find a photograph of yourself as a baby or small child. Either put it up on the wall or take a photo of it and keep it on your phone. That's you! Look at how awesome you are. Look at you with your dinky hands and tiny fingernails and squishy legs. A wonderful little being. Next time you speak to yourself harshly, bring this picture to mind and speak more kindly to yourself.

✦ Pay a visit to your inner child. Speak to your child self in a gentle voice. Tell them you'll take care of them and give them a hug. Then say, "You are enough." Let whatever comes up be and feel any emotions you may feel, then comfort your inner child again. This activity can help you to treat yourself with greater tenderness, to see who you really are and how far you've come.

✦ Pay a visit to your future self. Imagine yourself arriving at wherever you visualize living in your dream future. For example, whenever I've done this exercise, which I first learned from Tanis Frame of Decide to Thrive, I have visited my future self in a wooden cabin in the woods near a lake. Now see your future self opening the door to let your current self in and take a seat. Notice how calm your future self is and notice their reassuring smile. Imagine your future self telling you that whatever you are currently going through will pass and that you are going to be okay. Take that reassurance forward with you into your present life.

✦ Forgive yourself. Forgiveness is a way to be kind to yourself. Think about the events in your life that you feel guilty about. Is harbouring this guilt making you feel good? It's a destructive emotion, and it doesn't undo whatever you're feeling bad about, it only makes you feel sadder. So, make peace with yourself over it. Remind yourself that everybody makes mistakes, says hurtful things, behaves in ways they wish they hadn't and makes errors of judgement. What might you say to a friend you were helping to forgive themselves? You'd tell them what's done is done, you can't go back and change things. All you can do is learn from that event, apologize if you still need to, maybe write a letter of atonement if you feel it would help, and move on. Give yourself the same advice and take heed. Say, "I forgive myself" and explain why (for example, I was young and didn't think, but I've learned from this). Then feel the freedom of letting that guilt go.

When we live our lives through a lens of compassion, we become stronger and better equipped to cope with, and cherish, life in all its occasionally brutal glory, with its ups and downs, mistakes and joys and to remind ourselves at regular intervals that we really are enough.

Compassionate Curiosity

You aren't a better person for feeling guilty or bad about yourself, just a sadder one.

Jen Sincero

Life is a journey during which we can either be our own best ally or our own worst enemy. That depends on whether we see ourselves through a critical or a compassionate lens, from a position of judgement or one of acceptance.

It depends on whether we choose to believe the stories we tell ourselves or question them with gentle curiosity. It depends on whether we waste time concerning ourselves with what's outside our control or what's within our control. Only the latter enables us to join our own team, to see ourselves as good enough and live a life where we can truly flourish from where we are.

Personal growth can give our lives meaning. Yet in a world of perpetual pressure to strive and constantly improve, it can be difficult to strike a healthy balance between growth and gratitude, between self-improvement and self-acceptance, between betterment and contentment. For this reason, it's important to centre ourselves with compassionate curiosity.

For when we're compassionate and curious, we give ourselves the opportunity to live well-balanced and fulfilling lives. When we do that, we stop thinking about ourselves in terms of what we aren't and what we haven't and start thinking about ourselves in terms of what we are and what we have.

Assumptions are very easy to make and pretty hard to break. Assumptions close the doors to possibility whereas curiosity opens them. Only when we get curious about all the fictitious stories we've been telling ourselves for so long, can we gradually release external expectations and unshackle ourselves from society's shoulds. Thankfully, as a result of this process of unlearning, we can develop a healthy balanced view of ourselves and show up in the world authentically and confidently.

Only through this questioning can we rewrite the stories we've been telling ourselves about how enough we really are and rewire that outdated ancient wiring.

Only when we approach our self-perception and how we feel about ourselves with compassionate curiosity can we remove the pressures of perfection and the shackles of should and replace external validation with self-acceptance.

Only then can we replace imposter syndrome with self-belief, escape the comparison trap via compassionate truth and fight the "more war" with an attitude of gratitude.

Only then can we replace our inner critic with our inner cheerleader and replace our negativity bias with our joy detective. Only then can we find our happy medium.

As the central protagonists in our lives, in which we are either the hero or the victim, only when we curiously question the stories we tell ourselves can we rewrite the script. Curiosity trumps judgement, fear and criticism every time by increasing our self-awareness and helping us to become the authors, rather than the actors, of our own life stories.

Only with compassionate curiosity can we turn the inaccurate mental biopic that has been written by an external cast of scriptwriters into a more realistic narrative.

It's time to grab the pen back. Because

REFERENCES

1 Thomas Curran and Andrew P. Hill, "Perfectionism Is Increasing Over Time: A Meta-Analysis of Birth Cohort Differences From 1989 to 2016", *Psychological Bulletin*, 145, No. 4 (2019)

2 Annual report offers snapshot of U.S. college students' mental health needs, *Penn State News*, February 5 2015 https://news.psu.edu/story/343727/2015/02/05/research/annual-report-offers-snapshot-us-college-students%e2%80%99-mental-health

3 P. L. Hewitt and G. L. Flett, "Perfectionism in the Self and Social Contexts: Conceptualization, Assessment, and Association with Psychopathology", *Journal of Personality and Social Psychology*, 60:3 (1991)

4 Sylvia Ann Hewlett, Noni Allwood, Karen Sumberg and Sandra Scharf with Christina Fargnoli, "Cracking the Code: Executive Presence and Multicultural Professionals", Center for Talent Innovation (2013) www.talentinnovation.org/_private/assets/CrackingTheCode_EPMC-ExecSummFINAL-CTI.pdf

5 https://www.psychologytoday.com/gb/basics/social-comparison-theory

6 Pauline Rose Clance and Suzanne Imes, "The Imposter Phenomenon in High Achieving Women: Dynamics and Therapeutic Intervention", Georgia State University, *Psychotherapy Theory, Research and Practice*, 15:3 (Fall 1978)

7 R. W. Levenson *et al*, "Long-Term Marriage: Age, Gender, and Satisfaction", *Psychology and Aging*, American Psychological Association, 8:2 (1993)

8 Martin E. P. Seligman, *Flourish: A Visionary New Understanding of Happiness and Well-being* (Nicholas Brealey Publishing, 2011)

9 Hermann Heinrich Gossen, *The Laws of Human Relations and the Rules of Human Action Derived Therefrom* (MIT Press, 1954)

10 Thomas Gilovich, Amit Kumar, Lily Jampol, "A Wonderful Life: Experiential Consumption and the Pursuit of Happiness", *Journal of Consumer Psychology,* 25:1 (2015)

11 Barbara Fredrickson, *Positivity: Groundbreaking Research to Release Your Inner Optimist and Thrive* (One World Publications, 2011)

12 Christopher Peterson, Martin E. P. Seligman, "Character Strengths Before and After September 11", *Psychological Science,* 14 (2003)

13 Adam Grant, *Originals: How Non-Conformists Move the World* (WH Allen, 2016)

FURTHER READING

Glennon Doyle, *Untamed: Stop Pleasing, Start Living* (Vermillion, 2020)

Adam Grant, *Originals: How Non-Conformists Move the World* (W H Allen, 2016)

Louise L. Hay, *You Can Heal Your Life* (Hay House, 1984)

Alicia Keys, *More Myself: A Journey* (Macmillan, 2020)

Jennifer Pastiloff, *On Being Human: A Memoir of Waking Up, Living Real, and Listening Hard* (John Murray Learning, 2019)

Cheryl Rickman, *Navigating Loneliness: How to Connect with Yourself and Others – A Mental Health Handbook* (Trigger Publishing, 2021)

Jen Sincero, *You Are a Badass: How to Stop Doubting Your Greatness and Start Living an Awesome Life* (John Murray Learning, 2016)

Bronnie Ware, *The Top Five Regrets of the Dying: A Life Transformed by the Dearly Departed* (Hay House UK, 2012)

ACKNOWLEDGEMENTS

I'm forever grateful to all those who have my back and stand beside me, including my ancestors who, though no longer with me in person, stand behind me so I may have a "strong back, soft front and wild heart". Thank you to my parents, Denise and Roger Rickman. You were the best mother and father anyone could wish for and your endless, unconditional love and constant encouragement gave me the foundations from which to grow and allowed me to believe in myself.

Thank you to my friends and soul sisters for always making me feel good enough. I'm so grateful we are each other's cheerleaders in life, and always will be. Thanks to my darling Jennie, and to Ann, Peta, Lisa B and Ella, for always listening and supporting. Thank you Iva, Debra, Tanis, Annerose and all my D2T sisters, and Rebecca, Susan and Karen (my GLP sisters) for seeing, hearing, appreciating and encouraging me. Thank you to The Girlies, The Lotuses, The Poppies and my childhood friends, Karen and Helen for being in my life. And thank you to all those other people who encourage me via social media (you know who you are). You are enough! We are enough! And together, we've got this and we've got each other. Thank you to the team at Summersdale: Rebecca, Charlotte and Debbie, you've been wonderful to work with.

Finally, thank you to YOU – the person reading this book. I hope it has given you a boost in confidence so you can release those "shackles of should" and be happy being who you are. Because you really are wonderful enough. Thank you for being you!

ABOUT THE AUTHOR

Cheryl Rickman is a *Sunday Times* bestselling author and ghostwriter of 24 self-help, mental health and business books; a positive psychology practitioner and a Wellbeing Ambassador for the Network of Wellbeing.

After her parents' lives were cut short, Cheryl decided to devote her life to helping others to make the most of their own precious lives, through the books she writes and the workshops she gives. She specializes in writing empowering, practical books to help people fret less and flourish more.

Her most recent books include *Navigating Loneliness*, *The Happiness Bible* and *Be More Wonder Woman*. Having qualified with a certificate in Applied Positive Psychology in 2016, Cheryl also runs a well-being and rewilding project from a Hampshire woodland.

Cheryl lives with her husband, daughter and two Labradors in a country cottage in Hampshire, UK. She is a proud hugger of trees and lover of nature, has an overflowing bookshelf and her favourite colour is rainbow.

You can find out more at **www.CherylRickman.co.uk**

NOTES

NOTES

NOTES

NOTES

NOTES

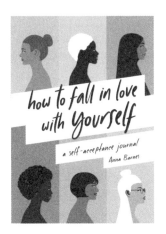

How to Fall in Love With Yourself
A Self-Acceptance Journal

Anna Barnes
£10.99
Paperback
ISBN: 978-1-78783-934-2

How to Be Perfectly Imperfect
Stop Comparing, Start Living

Candi Williams
£9.99
Paperback
ISBN: 978-1-78783-234-3

Be Kind to Your Mind
A Pocket Guide to Looking After Your Mental Health

Claire Chamberlain
£8.99
Hardback
ISBN: 978-1-78783-256-5

She Believed She Could So She Did
A Modern Woman's Guide to Life

Sam Lacey
£9.99
Paperback
ISBN: 978-1-78783-561-0

The Confidence Journal
Tips and Exercises to Help
You Overcome Self-Doubt

Anna Barnes
£9.99
Paperback
ISBN: 978-1-78783-305-0

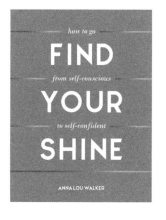

Find Your Shine
How to Go from Self-Conscious
to Self-Confident

Anna Lou Walker
£12.99
Hardback
ISBN: 978-1-78783-637-2

Have you enjoyed this book?
If so, why not write a review on your favourite website?

If you're interested in finding out more about
our books, find us on Facebook at **Summersdale
Publishers**, on Twitter at **@Summersdale** and
on Instagram at **@summersdalebooks**.

Thanks very much for buying this Summersdale book.

WWW.SUMMERSDALE.COM